Famous Women.

MARGARET FULLER.

MARGARET FULLER

(*MARCHESA OSSOLI*).

BY

JULIA WARD HOWE.

GREENWOOD PRESS, PUBLISHERS
WESTPORT, CONNECTICUT

Originally published in 1883
by Roberts Brothers, Boston

First Greenwood Reprinting 1970

Library of Congress Catalogue Card Number 69-13936

SBN 8371-4089-7

Printed in the United States of America

PREFATORY NOTE.

THE present volume bears the name of MARGARET FULLER simply, because it is by this name that its subject is most widely known and best remembered. Another name, indeed, became hers by marriage; but this later style and title were borne by our friend for a short period only, and in a country remote from her own. It was as Margaret Fuller that she took her place among the leading spirits of her time, and made her brave crusade against its unworthier features. The record of her brief days of wifehood and of motherhood is tenderly cherished by her friends, but the story of her life-work is best inscribed with the name which was hers by birth and baptism, the name which, in her keeping, acquired a significance not to be lost nor altered.

CONTENTS.

——◆——

CONTENTS.

MARGARET FULLER.

————◆————

CHAPTER I.

CHILDHOOD AND EARLY YOUTH. — SCHOOL DAYS.

THE subject of the following sketch, Sarah Margaret Fuller, has already been most fortunate in her biographers. Cut off herself in the prime of life, she left behind her devoted friends who were still in their full vigor of thought and sentiment. Three of these, James Freeman Clarke, Ralph Waldo Emerson, and William Henry Channing, set their hand, some thirty or more years ago, to the happy task of preserving for posterity their strong personal impressions of her character and influence. With these precious reminiscences were interwoven such extracts from her correspondence and diary as were deemed fittest to supply the outline of her own life and experience.

What, it may be asked, can such biographers have left for others to do? To surpass their work is not to be thought of. But, in the turning and perseverance of this planet, present soon becomes past, and that which has been best said asks to be said again. This biography, so rich in its suggestions and so valuable in its details, is already set in a past light by the progress of men and of things. Its theme has lost none of its interest. Nay, it is through the growing interest felt in Margaret and her work that a demand seems to have arisen for a later word about her, which cannot hope to be better or wiser than the words already made public, but which may borrow from them the inspiration for a new study and presentment.

According to the authorities already established, Sarah Margaret Fuller, the child of Timothy Fuller and Margaret Crane, was born at Cambridgeport, near Boston, on the 23d of May, 1810. She has herself given some account of her early life in an autobiographical sketch which forms the prelude to the work already published. Her father, she says, "was a lawyer and a politician," the son of a country clergyman, Harvard-bred both as to his college and his professional studies. She remembers him chiefly as absorbed in the business and interest of his profession, intent upon compassing the support of his family, and achieving such distinction as might prove compatible with that object. Her mother she describes as "one of those fair, flower-like natures, which sometimes spring up even beside the most dusty highways of life, — bound by one law with the blue sky, the dew, and the frolic birds." And in the arduous labor of her father's life, his love for this sweet mother " was the green spot on which he stood apart from the commonplaces of a mere bread-winning, bread-bestowing existence."

The case between Margaret and her father is the first to be disposed of in our consideration of her life and character. In the document just quoted from she does not paint him *en beau*. Here and elsewhere she seems to have been inclined to charge upon him the excessive study which exaggerated her natural precocity of temperament, and the Puritan austerity which brought her ungratified imagination into early conflict with the circumstances and surroundings of her start in life. In a brief preface to the memoir already published, a surviving brother of Margaret characterizes this view of the father as inadequate and unjust.

Margaret herself called her sketch an autobiographical romance, and evidently wrote it at a period of her life in which her personal experience had thrown little light upon the difficulties which parents encounter in the training of their children, and especially in that of their eldest-born.

From the sketch itself we gather that the Fuller household, although not corresponding to the dreams of its wonder-child, had yet in it elements which were most precious for her right growth and development. The family itself was descended from a stock deeply thoughtful and religious. With the impulses of such kindred came to Margaret the strict and thrifty order of primitive New England life, the absence of frivolity, the distaste for all that is paltry and superficial. In after years, her riper judgment must have shown her, as it has shown many, the value of these somewhat stern surroundings. The little Puritan children grew up, it is true, in the presence of a standard of character and of conduct which must have seemed severe to them. The results of such training have shown the world that the child so circumstanced will rise to the height of his teaching. Started on a solid and worthy plane of thought and of motive, he will not condescend to what is utterly mean, base, and trivial, either in motive or in act. If, as may happen, he fail in his first encounters with outside temptation, he will nevertheless severely judge his own follies, and will one day set himself to retrieve them with earnest diligence.

In the instance before us we can feel how bitter may have been the contrast between the child's natural tastes and the realities which surrounded her. Routine and restraint were burdensome to her when as yet she could not know their value. Not the less were they of great importance to her. The surroundings, too, which were devoid of artistic luxury and adornment, forced her to have recourse to the inner sense of beauty, which is sometimes lost and overlaid through much pleasing of the eye and ear.

Childhood, indeed, insists upon having the whole heavenly life unpacked upon the spot. Its to-day knows no to-morrow. Hence its common impatience and almost inevitable quarrel with the older generation, which in its eyes represents privation and correction.

The early plan of studies marked out for Margaret by her father was not devised by any commonplace mind. Mr. Fuller had gained from his own college life that love of culture which is valuable beyond any special attainment. His own scholarship had been more than common, and it became his darling object to transmit to his little daughter all that he himself had gained by study, and as much more as his circumstances would permit. He did indeed make the mistake, common in that day, of urging the tender intellect beyond the efforts proper to its stage of growth. Margaret says that the lessons

set for her were " as many and various as the
hours would allow, and on subjects far beyond
my age." These lessons were recited to her
father after office hours ; and as these hours
were often prolonged, the child's mind was kept
in a state of tension until long after the time
when the little head should have rested serenely
on its pillow. In consequence of this, it often
rested very ill, and the youthful prodigy of the
daytime was terrified at night by dreams and
illusions, and disturbed by sleep-walking. From
these efforts and excitements resulted, as she
says, "a state of being too active and too intense,
which wasted my constitution, and will bring
me, although I have learned to understand and
to regulate my now morbid temperament, to a
premature grave."

This was unhappy, certainly. The keen, active temperament did indeed acquire a morbid
intensity, and the young creature thus spurred
on to untimely effort began to live and to learn
at a pace with which the slowness of circumstance was never able to keep abreast.

Even with the allowance which must be made
for the notion of that time as to what a child
should be able to accomplish, it must grieve and
surprise us to find Margaret at the age of six
years engaged in the study of Latin and of
English grammar. Her father " demanded ac-

curacy and clearness in everything." Intelligible statement, reasoned thought, and a certainty which excluded all suppositions and reservations, — these were his requirements from his young pupil. A certain *quasi*-dogmatic mode of enunciation in later life, which may have seemed, on a superficial view, to indicate an undue confidence and assumption, had probably its origin in the decided way in which the little Margaret was taught to recite her lessons. Under the controlling influence of her father, she says that her own world sank deep within, away from the surface of her life : "In what I did and said I learned to have reference to other minds, but my true life was only the dearer that it was secluded and veiled over by a thick curtain of available intellect and that coarse but wearable stuff woven by the ages, common sense."

The Latin language opened for Margaet the door to many delights. The Roman ideal, definite and resolute, commended itself to her childish judgment ; and even in later life she recognized Virgil as worthy to lead the great Dante "through hell and to heaven." In Horace she enjoyed the serene and courtly appreciation of life ; in Ovid, the first glimpse of a mythology which carried her to the Greek Olympus. Her study "soon ceased to be a burden, and reading became a habit and a passion." Her first real friends she found in her father's book-closet, to which, in her leisure moments, she was allowed free access. Here, from a somewhat miscellaneous collection, she singled out the works of Shakespeare, Cervantes, and Molière, — " three great authors, all, though of unequal, yet of congenial powers ; all of rich and wide, rather than aspiring genius ; all free to the extent of the horizon their eye took in ; all fresh with impulse, racy with experience ; never to be lost sight of or superseded."

Of these three Shakespeare was the first in her acquaintance, as in her esteem. She was but eight years old when the interest of Romeo and Juliet led her to rebel against the discipline whose force she so well knew, and to persevere in reading before her father's very eyes a book forbidden for the Sabbath. For this offence she was summarily dismissed to bed, where her father, coming presently to expostulate with her, found her in a strangely impenitent state of mind.

Margaret's books thus supplied her imagination with the food which her outward surroundings did not afford. They did not, however, satisfy the cravings of her childish heart. These presently centred around a human object of intense interest, — a lady born and bred in polite European life, who brought something of its tone and atmosphere to cheer for a while the sombre New England horizon. Margaret seems to have first seen her at church, where the general aspect of things was especially distasteful to her.

"The puny child sought everywhere for the Roman or Shakespeare figures; and she was met by the shrewd, honest eye, the homely decency, or the smartness of a New England village on Sunday. There was beauty, but I could not see it then; it was not of the kind I longed for.

"As my eye one day was ranging about with its accustomed coldness, it was arrested by a face most fair, and well known, as it seemed at first glance; for surely I had met her before, and waited for her long. But soon I saw that she was an apparition foreign to that scene, if not to me. She was an English lady, who, by a singular chance, was cast upon this region for a few months."

This stranger seems to have been as gracious as she was graceful. Margaret, after this first glimpse, saw her often, sometimes at a neighbor's house, sometimes at her own. She was more and more impressed by her personal charm, which was heightened in the child's eyes by her accomplishments, rare in that time and place. The lady painted in oils and played on the harp. Margaret found the greatest delight in watching the growth of her friend's pictures, and in listening to her music. Better still, they walked together in the quiet of the country. "Like a guardian spirit, she led me through the fields and groves ; and every tree, every bird, greeted me and said, what I felt, 'She is the first angel of your life.'"

Delight so passionate led to a corresponding sorrow. The lady, who had tenderly responded to the child's mute adoration, vanished from her sight, and was thenceforth known to her only through the interchange of letters.

"When this friend was withdrawn," says Margaret, " I fell into a profound depression. Melancholy enfolded me in an atmosphere, as joy had done. This suffering, too, was out of the gradual and natural course. Those who are really children could not know such love or feel such sorrow." Her father saw in this depression a result of the too great isolation in which Margaret had thus far lived. He felt that she needed change of scene and, still more, intercourse with girls of her own age. The remedy proposed was that she should be sent to school, — a measure which she regarded with dread and dislike. She had hitherto found little pleasure in the society of other girls. She had sometimes joined the daughters of her neighbors in hard play, but had not felt herself at home with them. Her retired and studious life had, she says, given her "a cold aloofness," which could not predispose them in her favor. Despite her resistance, however, her father persevered in his intention, and Margaret became an inmate of the Misses Prescott's school in Groton, Mass.

Her experience here, though painful in some respects, had an important effect upon her after life.

At first her unlikeness to her companions was uncomfortable both to her and to them. Her exuberant fancy demanded outlets which the restraints of boarding-school life would not allow. The unwonted excitement produced by contact with other young people vented itself in fantastic acts, and freaks amusing but tormenting. The art of living with one's kind had not formed a part of Margaret's home education. Her nervous system had already, no doubt, been seriously disturbed by overwork.

Some plays were devised for the amusement of the pupils, and in these Margaret found herself entirely at home. In each of these the principal part was naturally assigned her, and the superiority in which she delighted was thus recognized. These very triumphs, however, in the end led to her first severe mortification, and on this wise: —

The use of rouge had been permitted to the girls on the occasion of the plays ; but Margaret was not disposed, when these were over, to relinquish the privilege, and continued daily to tinge her cheeks with artificial red. This freak suggested to her fellow-pupils an intended pleasantry, which awakened her powers of resentment to the utmost. Margaret came to the dinner-table, one day, to find on the cheeks of pupils and preceptress the crimson spot with which she had persisted in adorning her own. Suppressed laughter, in which even the servants shared, made her aware of the intended caricature. Deeply wounded, and viewing the somewhat personal joke in the light of an inflicted disgrace, Margaret's pride did not forsake her. She summoned to her aid the fortitude which some of her Romans had shown in trying moments, and ate her dinner quietly, without comment. When the meal was over she hastened to her own room, locked the door, and fell on the floor in convulsions. Here teachers and schoolfellows sorrowfully found her, and did their utmost to soothe her wounded feelings, and to efface by affectionate caresses the painful impression made by their inconsiderate fun.

Margaret recovered from this excitement, and took her place among her companions, but with an altered countenance and embittered heart.

She had given up her gay freaks and amusing inventions, and devoted herself assiduously to her studies. But the offence which she had received rankled in her breast. As not one of her fellow-pupils had stood by her in her hour of need, she regarded them as all alike perfidious and ungrateful, and, " born for love, now hated all the world."

This morbid condition of mind led to a result still more unhappy. Masking her real resentment beneath a calm exterior, Margaret received the confidences of her schoolfellows, and used their unguarded speech to promote discord among them. The girls, naturally enough, talked about each other, and said things which it would have been kind and wise not to repeat. Margaret's central position among them would have enabled her to reconcile their small differences and misunderstandings, which she, on the contrary, did her utmost to foment, not disdaining to employ misrepresentation in her mischievous mediation. Before long the spirit of discord reigned throughout the school, in which, the prime mover of the trouble tells us, " scarcely a peaceful affection or sincere intimacy remained." She had instinctively followed the ancient precept, " Divide et impera," and ruled for evil those who would have followed her for good.

This state of things probably became unbearable. Its cause was inquired into, and soon found. A tribunal was held, and before the whole school assembled, Margaret was accused of calumny and falsehood, and, alas! convicted of the same.

"At first she defended herself with self-possession and eloquence. But when she found that she could no more resist the truth, she suddenly threw herself down, dashing her head with all her force against the iron hearth, on which a fire was burning, and was taken up senseless."

All present were of course greatly alarmed at this crisis, which was followed, on the part of Margaret, by days of hopeless and apathetic melancholy. During these she would neither speak nor eat, but remained in a sort of stupor, — the result of conflicting emotions. In the pain which she now felt, her former resentment against her schoolmates disappeared. She saw only her own offence, and saw it without hope of being able to pass beyond it.

In this emergency, when neither the sorrow of her young companions nor the entreaties of her teachers seemed to touch her, a single friend was able to reach the seat of Margaret's distemper, and to turn the currents of her life once more into a healthful channel.

This lady, a teacher in the school, had always

felt a special interest in Margaret, whose character somewhat puzzled her. With the tact of true affection, she drew the young girl from the contemplation of her own failure, by narrating to her the circumstances which, through no fault of hers, had made her own life one of sorrow and of sacrifice.

Margaret herself, with a discernment beyond her years, had felt the high tone of this lady's character, and the "proud sensibility" expressed in her changing countenance. From her she could learn the lesson of hope and of comfort. Listening to the story, she no longer repulsed the hand of healing, but took patiently the soothing medicine offered by her visitor.

This story of Margaret's school life she herself has told, in an episode called "Marianna," which was published in her "Summer on the Lakes," and afterwards embodied in Mr. Clarke's contribution to the memoir already published. We have already quoted several passages from it, and will here give her account of the end of the whole matter.

"She returned to life, but it was as one who has passed through the valley of death. The heart of stone was quite broken in her; the fiery will fallen from flame to coal.

"When her strength was a little restored, she had all her companions summoned, and said to

them : ' I deserved to die, but a generous trust
has called me back to life.   I will be worthy
of the past, nor ever betray the trust, or re-
sent injury more.   Can you forgive the past ? '
And," says the narrative, " they not only for-
gave, but with love and earnest tears clasped
in their arms the returning sister.   They vied
with one another in offices of humble love to the
humbled one; and let it be recorded, as an instance of the pure honor of which young hearts
are capable, that these facts, known to some
forty persons, never, so far as I know, transpired
beyond those walls."

   In making this story public, we may believe
Margaret to have been actuated by a feeling of
the value of such an experience both in the study
of character and in the discipline of young minds.
Here was a girl, really a child in age, but already almost a woman in selfhood and imagination.   Untrained in intercourse with her peers in
age, she felt and exaggerated her own superiority
to those with whom her school life first brought
her in contact.   This superiority she felt impelled to assert and maintain.   So long as she
could queen it over the other pupils she was content.   The first serious wounding of her self-love
aroused in her a vengeful malignity, which grew
with its own exercise.   Unable as she found herself to command her little public by offices which

had seemed to her acts of condescension, she determined to rule through the evil principle of discord. In a fortunate moment she was arrested in this course by an exposure whose consequences showed her the reflection of her own misconduct in the minds of those around her. Extreme in all things, her self-reproach took the form of helpless despair, which yet, at the touch of true affection, gave way before the courageous determination to retrieve past error by future good desert.

The excellence of Margaret's judgment and the generosity of her heart appear in the effect which this fortunate failure had upon her maturer life. The pride of her selfhood had been overthrown. She had learned that she could need the indulgence and forgiveness of others, and had also learned that her mates, lightly esteemed by her up to that time, were capable of magnanimous forgiveness and generous rehabilitation. In the tender strength of her young mind, those impressions were so received that they were never thereafter effaced. The esteem of Margaret for her own sex, then rare in women of her order, and the great charity with which she ever regarded the offences of others, perhaps referred back through life to this time of trial, whose shortcoming was to be redeemed by such brilliant achievements.

Margaret's school days ended soon after this time, and she returned to her father's house, much instructed in the conditions of harmonious relations with her fellows.

CHAPTER II.

DR. HEDGE, a life-long friend of Margaret, has given a very interesting sketch of her in her girlhood. He first met her when he was a student at Harvard, and she a maiden of thirteen, in her father's house at Cambridge. Her precocity, mental and physical, was such that she passed for a much older person, and had already a recognized place in society. She was at this time in blooming and vigorous health, with a tendency to over-stoutness, which, the Doctor thinks, gave her some trouble. She was not handsome nor even pretty, but her animated countenance at once made its own impression, and awakened in those who saw her a desire to know more of her. Fine hair and teeth, vivacious eyes, and a peculiarly graceful carriage of the head and neck were points which redeemed her from the charge of plainness. This face of hers was, indeed, somewhat problematic in its expression, which carried with it the assurance of great possibilities, but not the certainty of their fulfilment.   Her conversation was already brilliant and full of interest, with a satirical turn which became somewhat modified in after life. Dr. Hedge fixes her stay in the Groton school at the years 1824, 1825, and mentions her indulgence in sarcasm as a source of trouble to her in a school earlier attended, that of Dr. Park, of Boston.

In the year 1826 his slight acquaintance with her grew into a friendship which, as we have said, ended only with her life.   During the seven years that followed he had abundant occasion to note her steady growth and the intensity of her inner life.   This was with her, as with most young persons, "a period of romance and of dreams, of yearning and of passion."   He thinks that she did not at this time pursue any systematic study.   " She read with the heart, and was learning more from social experience than from books."   One leading trait of her life was already prominent.   This was a passionate love of all beauties, both in nature and in art.

If not corresponding to a scholar's idea of systematic study, Margaret's pursuit of culture in those years must have been arduous and many-sided.   This we may partly gather from the books named and the themes touched upon in her correspondence with the beloved teacher who had brought her such near and tender help in her hour of need. To this lady, in a letter dated July 11, 1825, Margaret rehearses the routine of her daily life : —

" I rise a little before five, walk an hour, and then practise on the piano till seven, when we breakfast. Next I read French, Sismondi's ' Literature of the South of Europe,' till eight, then two or three lectures in Brown's Philosophy. About half-past nine I go to Mr. Perkins's school and study Greek till twelve, when, the school being dismissed, I recite, go home, and practise again till dinner, at two. Sometimes, if the conversation is very agreeable, I lounge for half an hour over the dessert, though rarely so lavish of time. Then, when I can, I read two hours in Italian, but I am often interrupted. At six I walk or take a drive. Before going to bed I play or sing for half an hour, and about eleven retire to write a little while in my journal, — exercises on what I have read, or a series of characteristics which I am filling up according to advice."

A year later she mentions studying " Madame de Staël, Epictetus, Milton, Racine, and Castilian ballads, with great delight." She asks her correspondent whether she would rather be the brilliant De Staël or the useful Edgeworth. In 1827 we find her occupied with a critical study of the elder Italian poets. She now mentions Miss Francis (Lydia Maria Child) as her intended companion in a course of metaphysical study.   She characterizes this lady as " a natural person, a most rare thing in this age of cant and pretension.   Her conversation is charming ; she brings all her powers to bear upon it.   Her style is varied, and she has a very pleasant and spirited way of thinking."

Margaret's published correspondence with her dear teacher ends in 1830, with these words : —

" My beloved supporter in those sorrowful hours, can I ever forget that to your treatment in that crisis of youth I owe the true life, the love of Truth and Honor ? "

From these years of pedagogy and of patience we must now pass to the time when this bud, so full of promise, unfolded into a flower rare and wondrous.

The story of Margaret's early studies, and the wide reach of her craving for knowledge, already mark her as a creature of uncommon gifts.   A devourer of books she had been from the start ; but books alone could not content this ardent mind, at once so critical and so creative.   She must also have life at first-hand, and feed her intelligence from its deepest source.   Hence the long story of her friendships, so many and various, yet so earnest and efficient.

What the chosen associates of this wonderful

woman have made public concerning the interest of her conversation and the value of her
influence tasks to the utmost the believing
powers of a time in which the demon of self-
interest seems to unfold himself out of most of
the metamorphic flowers of society. Margaret
and her friends might truly have said, " Our
kingdom is not of this world," — at least, according to what this world calls kingly. But what
imperial power had this self-poised soul, which
could so widely open its doors and so closely
shut them, which could lead in its train the
brightest and purest intelligences, and " bind the
sweet influences " of starry souls in the garland
of its happy hours! And here we may say,
her kingdom was not *all* of this world ; for the
kingdom of noble thought and affection is in this
world and beyond it, and the real and ideal are
at peace within its bounds.

In the divided task of Margaret's biography
it was given to James Freeman Clarke to speak
of that early summer of her life in which these
tender and intimate relations had their first and
most fervent unfolding. The Harvard student
of that day was probably a personage very unlike
the present revered pastor of the Church of the
Disciples. Yet we must believe that the one
was graciously foreshadowed in the other, and

that Margaret found in him the germ of what
the later world has learned so greatly to respect
and admire.

The acquaintance between these two began
in 1829, and was furthered by a family connection which Margaret, in one of her early letters,
playfully characterized as a cousinship in the
thirty-seventh degree.

During the four years immediately following,
the two young people either met or corresponded
daily. In explaining the origin of this friendship, Mr. Clarke modestly says : —

"She needed a friend to whom to speak of
her studies, to whom to express the ideas which
were dawning and taking shape in her mind.
She accepted me for this friend ; and to me it
was a gift of the gods, an influence like no
other."

This intercourse was at first on both sides an
entertainment sought and found. In its early
stages Margaret characterizes her correspondent
as "a socialist by vocation, a sentimentalist by
nature, and a Channing-ite from force of circumstance and of fashion." Further acquaintance
opened beneath the superficial interest the
deeper sources of sympathy, and a valued letter
from Margaret is named by Mr. Clarke as
having laid the foundation of a friendship to
which he owed both intellectual enlightenment

and spiritual enlargement. More than for these he thanks Margaret for having imparted to him an impulse which carried him bravely forward in what has proved to be the normal direction of his life. Although destined, after those early years of intimate communion, to live far apart and in widely different spheres of labor and of interest, the regard of the two friends never suffered change or diminution.

And here we come upon a governing feature in Margaret's intercourse with her friends. She had the power of leading those who interested her to a confidence which unfolded to her the deepest secrets of their life. Now came in play that unexplained action of one mind upon another which we call personal magnetism, and which is more distinctly recognized to-day than in other times as an element in social efficiency. It is this power which, united with intellectual force, gives leadership to individual men, and enables the great orator to hold a mighty audience in the hollow of his hand.

With Margaret at the period we speak of the exercise of this power was intensive rather than extensive. The circumstances of the time had something to do with this. Here was a soul whose objects and desires boldly transcended the sphere of ordinary life. It could neither wholly contain nor fitly utter itself. Pulpit and platform were then interdicted to her sex. The mimic stage, had she thought of it, would have mocked her with its unreality. On single souls, one at a time, she laid her detaining grasp, and asked what they could receive and give. Something noble she must perceive in them before she would condescend to this parley. She did not insist that her friends should possess genius; but she could only make friends of those who, like herself, were seekers after the higher life. Worthiness of object commended even mediocrity to her; but shallow worldliness awakened her contempt.

In the exercise of this discrimination she no doubt sometimes gave offence. Mr. Clarke acknowledges that she not only seemed, but was, haughty and supercilious to the multitude, while to the chosen few she was the very embodiment of tender and true regard.

It must also be acknowledged that this same magnetism which attracted some persons so strongly was to others as strongly repellent. Where she was least known this repulsion was most felt. It yielded to admiration and esteem where acquaintance went beyond the mere recognition of Margaret's air and manner, which made a stranger a little uncertain whether he would be amicably entertained or subjected to a *reductio ad absurdum.* As in any community impressions of personality are more likely to be superficial than thorough, it is probable that a very general misunderstanding which, at a later day, grew up between Margaret and the great world of a small New England city had its origin in a misconstruction of her manner when among strangers, or on the occasion of a first introduction. To recall this shallow popular judgment of her is not pleasant, but some mention of it does belong to any summary of her life. With such friends as she had, she had no reason to look upon herself as one who was neither understood nor appreciated. Yet her heart, which instinctively sought the empire of universal love, may have been grieved at the indifference and dislike which she sometimes encountered. Those who know how, in some circles, her name became a watchword for all that was eccentric and pretentious in the womanhood of her day, will smile or sigh at the contrast between the portraitures of Margaret given in the volumes of the memoir and the caricature of her which was current in the mind of the public at large.

These remarks anticipate the pains and distinctions of a later period. For the present let us confine our attention to the happy days at Cambridge, which Margaret may not have recognized as such, but which must have seemed bright to her when contrasted with the years of labor and anxiety which followed them.

Mr. Clarke tells us that Margaret and he began the study of the German language in 1832, moved thereunto by Thomas Carlyle's brilliant exposition of the merits of leading German authors. In three months' time Margaret had acquired easy command of the language, and within the year had read the most important works of Goethe and Schiller, with the writings also of Tieck, Körner, Richter, and Novalis. Extracts from her letters at this time show that this extensive reading was neither hasty nor superficial.

She finds herself happier in the companionship of Schiller than in that of Goethe, of whom she says, " That perfect wisdom and merciless reason seem cold after those seducing pictures of forms more beautiful than truth." The " Elective Affinities " suggests to her various critical questions, but does not carry her away with the sweep of its interest. From "the immense superiority of Goethe" she finds it a relief to turn to the simplicity of Novalis, "a wondrous youth, who has written only one volume," and whose "one-sidedness, imperfection, and glow seem refreshingly human" to her. Körner becomes a fixed star in the heaven of her thought. Lessing interests her less. She credits him with the production of "well conceived and sustained characters and interesting situations," but not with any profound knowledge of human nature. "I think him easily followed; strong, but not deep."

This was with Margaret, as Dr. Hedge has well observed, the period of romance. Her superiority to common individuals appeared in the fact that she was able to combine with intense personal aspirations and desires a wide outlook into the destinies of the human race.

We find her, in these very days, "engaged in surveying the level on which the public mind is poised." She turns from the poetic tragedy and comedy of life to study, as she says, "the rules of its prose," and to learn from the talk of common people what elements and modes of thought go to make up the average American mind. She listens to George Thompson, the English anti-slavery orator, and is led to say that, if she had been a man, she should have coveted the gift of eloquence above all others, and this for the intensity of its effects. She thinks of writing six historical tragedies, and devises the plan for three of them. Tales of Hebrew history it is also in her mind to compose. Becoming convinced that "some fixed opinion on the subject of metaphysics is an essential aid to systematic culture," she addresses herself to the study of Fichte and Jacobi, of Brown and Stewart. The first of these appeared to her incomprehensible. Of the second, she conjectures that his views are derived from some author whom she has not read. She thinks in good earnest of writing a life of Goethe, and wishes to visit Europe in order to collect the material requisite for this. Her appreciation of Dr. Channing is shown in a warm encomium on his work treating of slavery, of which she says, " It comes like a breath borne over some solemn sea which separates us from an island of righteousness."

In summing up his account of this part of Margaret's life, Mr. Clarke characterizes self-culture as the object in which she was content to lose sight of all others. Her devotion to this great end was, he says, " wholly religious, and almost Christian." She was religious in her recognition of the divine element in human experience, and Christian in her elevation above the sordid interests of life, and in her devotion to the highest standards of duty and of destiny. He admits, however, that her aim, noble as it was, long remained too intensely personal to reach the absolute generosity required by the Christian rule. This defect made itself felt outwardly by a certain disesteem of " the vulgar herd," and in an exaggerated worship of great personalities. Its inner effects were more serious. To her darling desire for growth and development she sacrificed "everything but manifest duty." The want of harmony between her outward circumstances and her inward longings so detained her thoughts that she was unable to pass beyond the confines of the present moment, and could not foresee that true growth must bring her, as it soon did, a great enlargement of influence and relation.

CHAPTER III.

RELIGIOUS BELIEFS.—MARGARET'S EARLY CRITICS.
— FIRST ACQUAINTANCE WITH MR. EMERSON.

IT was to be expected that in such a correspondence as that between Margaret and James
Freeman Clarke the chord of religious belief
would not remain untouched. From Margaret's own words, in letters and in her journal,
we clearly gather that her mind, in this respect,
passed through a long and wide experience.
Fortunate for her was, in that day, the Unitarian pulpit, with its larger charity and freer exe-
gesis. With this fold for her spiritual home,
she could go in and out, finding pasture, while
by the so-called Orthodox sects she would have
been looked upon as standing without the bounds
of all religious fellowship.

The requirements of her nature were twofold.
A religious foundation for thought was to her
a necessity. Equally necessary was to her the
untrammelled exercise of critical judgment, and
the thinking her own thoughts, instead of accepting those of other people. We may feel sure
that Margaret, even to save her own soul, would

not and could not have followed any confession
of faith in opposition to her own best judgment.
She would have preferred the hell of the free
soul to the heaven of the slave. To combine
this intellectual interpretation of religious duty
with the simple devotion which the heart craves
is not easy for any one. We may be very glad
to find that for her it was not impossible. Her
attitude between these two points of opposition
is indeed edifying; for, while she follows thought
with the daring of a sceptic, and fearlessly reasons concerning the highest mysteries, she yet
acknowledges the insufficiency of human knowledge for themes so wonderful, and here, as
nowhere else, bows her imperial head and confesses herself human.

One thing we may learn from what Margaret
has written on this subject, if we do not already
know it, and this is, that in any true religious
experience there must be progress and change
of attitude. This progress may be first initiated
by the preponderance of thought or by that of
affection, but, as it goes on, the partiality of
first views will be corrected by considerations
which are developed by later study. Religious
sincerity is, in the end, justified in all its stages;
but these stages, separately considered, will appear more or less incomplete and sometimes even
irreligious.

When first interrogated by her correspondent, she says : " I have determined not to form settled opinions at present. Loving or feeble natures need a positive religion, a visible refuge, a protection, as much in the passionate season of youth as in those stages nearer to the grave. But mine is not such. My pride is superior to any feelings I have yet experienced ; my affection is strong admiration, not the necessity of giving or receiving assistance or sympathy." So much for the subjective side of the matter with Margaret at this time. The objective is formulated by her in this brief creed : " I believe in Eternal Progression. I believe in a God, a Beauty and Perfection to which I am to strive all my life for assimilation. From these two articles of belief I draw the rules by which I strive to regulate my life. Tangible promises, well-defined hopes, are things of which I do not now feel the need. At present my soul is intent on this life, and I think of religion as its rule."

Those last words are not in contrast with the general tone of religious teaching to-day, but when Margaret wrote them to James Freeman Clarke, an exaggerated adjournment of human happiness to the glories of another world was quite commonly considered as essential to a truly Christian standpoint.

Even at this self-sufficing period of her life Margaret's journals were full of prayer and aspiration. Here are some of the utterances of this soul, which she herself calls a proud one : " Blessed Father, nip every foolish wish in blossom. Lead me any way to truth and goodness, but if it might be, I would not pass from idol to idol. Let no mean sculpture deform a mind disorderly, perhaps ill-furnished, but spacious and life-warm."

After hearing a sermon on the nature of duties, social and personal, she says : " My heart swelled with prayer. I began to feel hope that time and toil might strengthen me to despise the ' vulgar parts of felicity,' and live as becomes an immortal creature. Oh, lead me, my Father ! root out false pride and selfishness from my heart ; inspire me with virtuous energy, and enable me to improve every talent for the eternal good of myself and others."

Seasons of bitter discouragement alternated at this time with the moments in which she felt, not only her own power, but also the excellence of her aims in life.

Of one of these dark hours Margaret's journal gives a vivid description, from which some passages may be quoted. The occasion was a New England Thanksgiving, a day on which her attendance at church was almost compulsory.

This church was not to her a spiritual home, and on the day now spoken of the song of thanksgiving made positive discord in her ears. She felt herself in no condition to give thanks. Her feet were entangled in the problem of life. Her soul was agonized by its unreconciled contradictions.

" I was wearied out with mental conflicts. I felt within myself great power and generosity and tenderness ; but it seemed to me as if they were all unrecognized, and as if it was impossible that they should be used in life. I was only one-and-twenty ; the past was worthless, the future hopeless ; yet I could not remember ever voluntarily to have done a wrong thing, and my aspiration seemed very high."

Looking about in the church, she envied the little children for their sense of dependence and protection. She knew not, she says, " that none could have any father but God," knew not that she was "not the only lonely one, the selected Œdipus, the special victim of an iron law."

From this intense and exaggerated self-consciousness, the only escape was in fleeing from self. She sought to do this, as she had often done, by a long quick walk, whose fatigue should weary out her anguish, and enable her to return home " in a state of prayer." On this day this resource did not avail her.

"All seemed to have reached its height. It seemed as if I could never return to a world in which I had no place, to the mockery of humanities. I could not act a part, nor seem to live any longer."

The aspect of the outer world was in correspondence with these depressing thoughts.

"It was a sad and sallow day of the late autumn. Slow processions of clouds were passing over a cold blue sky ; the hues of earth were dull and gray and brown, with sickly struggles of late green here and there. Sometimes a moaning gust of wind drove late, reluctant leaves across the path—there was no life else." Driven from place to place by the conflict within her, she sat down at last to rest "where the trees were thick about a little pool, dark and silent. All was dark, and cold, and still." Suddenly the sun broke through the clouds "with that transparent sweetness, like the last smile of a dying lover, which it will use when it has been unkind all a cold autumn day." And with this unlooked-for brightness passed into her soul "a beam from its true sun," whose radiance, she says, never departed more. This sudden illumination was not, however, an unreasoning, unaccountable one. In that moment flashed upon her the solution of the problem of self, whose perplexities had followed her from her childish days.

She comprehended at once the struggle in which she had been well-nigh overcome, and the illusion which had till then made victory impossible. " I saw how long it must be before the soul can learn to act under these limitations of time and space and human nature; but I saw also that it must do it.   I saw there was no self, that selfishness was all folly, and the result of circumstance; that it was only because I thought self real that I suffered; that I had only to live in the idea of the all, and all was mine.   This truth came to me, and I received it unhesitatingly; so that I was for that hour taken up into God. . . . My earthly pain at not being recognized never went deep after this hour.   I had passed the extreme of passionate sorrow, and all check, all failure, all ignorance, have seemed temporary ever since."

The progress of this work already brings us to that portion of Margaret's life in which her character was most likely to be judged of by the world around her as already determined in its features and aspect.   That this judgment was often a misjudgment is known to all who remember Margaret's position in Boston society in the days of her lessons and conversations.   A really vulgar injustice was often done her by those who knew of her only her appearance and supposed pretensions.   Those to whom she

never was a living presence may naturally ask
of those who profess to have known her, whether
this injustice did not originate with herself,
whether she did not do herself injustice by ha-
bitually presenting herself in an attitude which
was calculated to heighten the idea, already conceived, of her arrogance and overweening self-
esteem.

Independently of other sources of information,
the statements of one so catholic and charitable
as Mr. Emerson meet us here, and oblige us to
believe that the great services which Margaret
was able to render to those with whom she came
into relation were somewhat impaired by a self-
esteem which it would have been unfortunate
for her disciples to imitate. The satirists of the
time saw this, and Margaret, besides encounter-
ing the small-shot of society ridicule, received
now and then such a broadside as James Russell
Lowell gave her in his " Fable for Critics." Of
this long and somewhat bitter tirade a few lines
may suffice as a specimen : —

" But here comes Miranda. Zeus ! where shall I flee to ?
She has such a *penchant* for bothering me, too !
She always keeps asking if I don't observe a
Particular likeness 'twixt her and Minerva.

     .   .   .   .   .

She will take an old notion and make it her own,
By saying it o'er in her sibylline tone ;

Or persuade you 't is something tremendously deep,
By repeating it so as to put you to sleep ;
And she well may defy any mortal to see through it,
When once she has mixed up her infinite *me* through it.

    .   .   .   .   .

Here Miranda came up and said : Phœbus, you know
That the infinite soul has its infinite woe,
As I ought to know, having lived cheek by jowl,
Since the day I was born, with the infinite soul."

These remarks, explanatory and apologetic,
are suggested partly by Mr. Emerson's statements concerning the beginning of his acquaintance with Margaret, and partly by the writer's
own recollections of the views of outsiders concerning her, which contrasted strongly with the
feeling and opinion of her intimates.

Mr. Emerson first heard of Margaret from
Dr. Hedge, and afterwards from Miss Martineau. Both were warm in their praise of her,
and the last-named was especially desirous to
introduce her to Mr. Emerson, whom she very
much wished to know. After one or more chance
meetings, it was arranged that Margaret should
spend a fortnight with Mrs. Emerson. The
date of this visit was in July, 1836.

To the description of her person already quoted
from Dr. Hedge, we may add a sentence or two
from Mr. Emerson's record of his first impressions of her : —

" She had a face and frame that would indi-

cate fulness and tenacity of life. . . . She was
then, as always, carefully and becomingly dressed,
and of lady-like self-possession. For the rest,
her appearance had nothing prepossessing. Her
extreme plainness, a trick of incessantly opening
and shutting her eyelids, the nasal tone of her
voice, all repelled ; and I said to myself, we shall
never get far."

But Margaret greatly esteemed Mr. Emerson,
and was intent upon establishing a friendly relation with him. Her reputation for satire was
well known to him, and was rather justified in
his eyes by the first half-hour of her conversation with him.

" I believe I fancied her too much interested
in personal history ; and her talk was a comedy
in which dramatic justice was done to every-
body's foibles. I remember that she made me
laugh more than I liked."

Passing into a happier vein, she unfolded her
brilliant powers of repartee, expressed her own
opinions, and sought to discover those of her
companion. Soon her wit had effaced the impression of her personal unattractiveness ; "and
the eyes, which were so plain at first, swam with
fun and drolleries, and the very tides of joy and
superabundant life." He now saw that "her
satire was only the pastime and necessity of
her talent," and as he learned to know her

better, her plane of character rose constantly in his estimation, disclosing "many moods and powers, in successive platforms or terraces, each above each."

Mr. Emerson likens Margaret's relations with her friends to the wearing of a necklace of social brilliants of the first water. A dreaded waif among the merely fashionable, her relations with men and women of higher tastes were such that, as Mr. Emerson says, "All the art, the thought, and the nobleness in New England seemed at that moment related to her, and she to it."

In the houses of such friends she was always a desired guest, and in her various visitings she "seemed like the queen of some parliament of love, who carried the key to all confidences, and to whom every question had been referred."

Mr. Emerson gives some portraits which make evident the variety as well as the extent of Margaret's attraction. Women noted for beauty and for social talent, votaries of song, students of art and literature, — men as well as women, — vied with each other in their devotion to her. To each she assumed and sustained a special relation whose duties and offices she never neglected nor confounded. To each she became at once a source of inspiration and a court of appeal. The beneficence of her influence may be inferred from the lasting gratitude of her friends, who always remembered her as having wisely guided and counselled them.

Any human life is liable to be modified by the supposition that its results are of great interest to some one whose concern in them is not a selfish one. Where this supposition is verified by corresponding acts, the power of the individual is greatly multiplied. This merciful, this providential interest Margaret felt for each of her many friends. There was no illusion in the sense of her value which they, all and severally, entertained.

Where, we may ask, shall we look to-day for a friendliness so wide and so availing? We can only answer that such souls are not sent into the world every day. Few of us can count upon inspiring even in those who are nearest and dearest to us this untiring concern in our highest welfare. But such a friend to so many it would be hard to find.

When we consider Margaret's love of literature, and her power of making its treasures her own, we must think of this passion of hers for availing intercourse with other minds as indeed a providential gift which no doubt lavished in passing speech much that would have been eloquent on paper, but which evidently had on society the immediate and intensified effect which distinguishes the living word above the dead letter.

CHAPTER IV.

MARGARET'S enthusiasm for art was in some
measure the result of her study of Goethe. Yet
she had in herself a love of the beautiful, and a
sense of its office in life, which would naturally
have led her far in the direction in which this
great master gave her so strong an impulsion.
In her multifarious reading she gave much time
to the literature of art, and in those days had
read everything that related to Michael Angelo
and Raphael, Quatremère de Quincy, Condivi,
Vasari, Benvenuto Cellini, and others. The
masters themselves she studied in the casts of
the Boston Athenæum, in the Brimmer Collection of Engravings, and in the contents of
certain portfolios which a much-esteemed friend
placed at her service, and which contained all
the designs of Michael and Raphael.

The delight which Margaret felt in these
studies demanded the sympathy of her elect
associates, and Mr. Emerson remembers cer-

tain months as having been "colored with the genius of these Italians." In 1839 Mr. Allston's numerous works were collected for a public exhibition which drew to Boston lovers of art from many distant places. In the same year some sculptures of Greenough and Crawford were added to the attractions of the Boston Athenæum.

In Margaret's appreciation of these works, if we may believe Mr. Emerson, a certain fanciful interpretation of her own sometimes took the place of a just estimate of artistic values. Yet he found her opinion worthy of attention, as evincing her real love of beautiful things, and her great desire to understand the high significance of art. He makes some quotations from her notes on the Athenæum Gallery of sculpture in 1840.

Here she finds marble busts of Byron and Napoleon. The first, with all its beauty, appears to her "sultry, stern, all-craving, all-commanding," and expressive of something which accounts for what she calls "the grand failure of his scheme of existence." The head of Napoleon is, she says, not only stern but ruthless. "Yet this ruthlessness excites no aversion. The artist has caught its true character, and given us here the Attila, the instrument of fate to serve a purpose not his own." She groups the poet and

the warrior together as having, "the one in letters, the other in arms, represented more fully
than any other the tendency of their time;
[they] more than any other gave it a chance
for reaction." Near these she finds a head of
the poet Ennius, and busts also of Edward
Everett, Washington Allston, and Daniel Webster. Her comment upon this juxtaposition is
interesting.

"Yet even near the Ennius and Napoleon
our American men look worthy to be perpet-
uated in marble or bronze, if it were only for
their air of calm, unpretending sagacity."

Mr. Henry James, Jr., writing of Nathaniel
Hawthorne, speaks of the Massachusetts of
forty or more years ago as poor in its æsthetic
resources. Works of art indeed were then few
in number, and decorative industry, in its present extent, was not dreamed of. But in the
intellectual form of appreciative criticism the
Boston of that day was richer than the city of
our own time. The first stage of culture is
cultivation, and the art lovers of that day had
sowed the seed of careful study, and were intent
upon its growth and ripening. If possession is
nine points of the law, as it is acknowledged
to be, the knowledge of values may be said to
be nine points of possession, and Margaret and
her friends, with their knowledge of the import

of art, and with their trained and careful observation of its outward forms, had a richer feast in the casts and engravings of that time than can be enjoyed to-day by the amateur, who, with a *bric-a-brac* taste and *blasé* feeling, haunts the picture-shops of our large cities, or treads the galleries in which the majestic ghosts of earnest times rebuke his flippant frivolity.

We have lingered over these records of Margaret's brilliant youth, because their prophecies aid us greatly in the interpretation of her later life. The inspired maiden of these letters and journals is very unlike the "Miss Fuller" who in those very days was sometimes quoted as the very embodiment of all that is ungraceful and unfeminine. How little were the beauties of her mind, the graces of her character, guessed at or sought for by those who saw in her unlikeness to the popular or fashionable type of the time matter only for derisive comment!

It may not be unimportant for us here to examine a little the *rationale* of Margaret's position, and inquire whether the trait which occasioned so much animadversion was not the concomitant of one of Margaret's most valuable qualities. This we should call a belief in her own moral and intellectual power, which impelled her to examine and decide all questions for herself, and which enabled her to accomplish many a brave work and sacrifice. This sense of her own power was answered by the common confession of weakness which then was, and still is, a part of the received creed of women on the level of good society. Did not the prone and slavish attitude of these women appear to Margaret as fatal to character as it really is ?

"I am only a woman," was a remark often heard in that day, as in this, from women to whom that "only" was not to be permitted ! Only the guardian of the beginning of life, only the sharer in all its duties and inspirations ? Culture and Christianity recognized as much as this, but the doctrine still remained an abstract one, and equal rights were scarcely thought of as a corollary to equal duties. Margaret never saw, though she foresaw, the awakening and recognition of the new womanhood which is already changing the aspect of civilized society. An eccentric in her own despite, she had dared assume her full height, and to demand her proper place. Her position was as exceptional as was her genius. From the isolation of her superiority, was it wonderful that she should consider it more absolute than it really was ?

This exaggerated sense of power is perhaps nothing more than the intensification of consciousness which certain exigencies will awaken in those who meet them with a special work to do and a special gift to do it with. It must be remembered that Margaret's self-esteem did not really involve any disesteem of others. She honored in all their best traits, and her only ground of quarrel with humanity at large was its derogation from its own dignity, its neglect of its own best interests. Such a sense of human value as she possessed was truly a Christian gift, and it was in virtue of this that she was able to impart such exhilaration and hopefulness to those who were content to learn of her.

But here, in our chronicle, the early morning hours are already over. The inward conquest which was sealed by the sunbeam of that " sallow" November day becomes the prelude to an outward struggle with difficulties which tasked to the utmost the strength acquired by our neophyte through prayer and study.

In the spring of 1833 Margaret found herself obliged to leave the academic shades of Cambridge for the country retirement of Groton. Her father, wearied with a long practice of the law, had removed his residence to the latter place, intending to devote his later years to literary labor and the education of his younger children. To Margaret this change was unwelcome, and the result showed it, at a later day, to have been unfortunate for the family. She did not, however, take here the position of a malcontent,

4

but that of one who, finding herself removed from congenial surroundings, knows how to summon to her aid the hosts of noble minds with which study has made her familiar. Her German books go with her, and Goethe, Schiller, and Jean Paul solace her lonely hours. She reads works on architecture, and books of travel in Italy, while sympathy with her father's pursuits leads her to interest herself in American history, concerning which he had collected much information with a view to historical composition.

We find her also engaged in tuition. She has four pupils, probably the younger children of the family, and gives lessons in three languages five days in the week, besides teaching geography and history. She has much needlework to do, and the ill-health of her mother and grandmother brings additional cares. The course of study which she has marked out for herself can only be pursued, she says, on three evenings in the week, and at chance hours in the day. It includes a careful perusal of Alfieri's writings and an examination into the evidences of the Christian religion. To this she is impelled by "distressing sceptical notions" of her own, and by the doubts awakened in her mind by the arguments of infidels and of deists, some of whom are numbered among her friends.

The following letter, addressed by Margaret to

a much-admired friend, will give us some idea
of the playful mood which relieved her days of
serious application.

"GROTON, 1834.

" To Mrs. ALMIRA B.

" Are you not ashamed, O most friendshipless
clergywoman ! not to have enlivened my long
seclusion by one line ? Does the author of the
' lecture delivered with much applause before the
Brooklyn Lyceum ' despise and wish to cast off
the author of ' essays contumeliously rejected by
that respected publication, the " Christian Ex-
aminer " ? ' That a little success should have
such power to steel the female heart to base
ingratitude ! O Ally ! Ally ! wilt thou forget
that it was I (in happier hours thou hast full oft
averred it) who first fanned the spark of thy
ambition into flame ? Think'st thou that thou
owest naught to those long sweeps over the in-
expressive realities of literature, when thou wast
obliged to trust to my support, thy own opinions
as yet scarce budding from thy heels or shoulders ? Dost thou forget — but my emotions will
not permit me to pursue the subject ; surely I
must have jogged your conscience sufficiently.
I shall follow the instructions of the great
Goethe, and, having in some degree vented my
feelings, address you as if you were what you
ought to be. Still remains enveloped in mys-

tery the reason why neither you nor my reverend friend came to bid me good-by before I left your city, according to promise. I suspected the waiter at the time of having intercepted your card ; but your long venomous silence has obliged me to acquit him. I had treasured up sundry little anecdotes touching my journey homeward, which, if related with dramatic skill, might excite a smile on your face, O laughter-loving blue-stocking ! I returned home under the protection of a Mr. Fullerton, fresh from London and Paris, who gave me an entirely new view of continental affairs. He assured me that the German Prince[1] was an ignorant pretender, in the face of my assurances that I had read and greatly admired his writings, and gave me a contemptuous description of Waldo Emerson *dining in boots* at Timothy Wiggin's, *absolument à faire mourir !* All his sayings were exquisite. And then a *sui generis mother* whom I met with on board the steamboat. All my pretty pictures are blotted out by the rude hand of Time : verily this checking of speech is dangerous. If all the matter I have been preserving for various persons is in my head, packed away, distributed among the various organs, how immensely will my head be developed when I return to the world. This is the first time in my

[1] Pückler-Muskau.

life that I have known what it is to have nobody to speak to, *c'est à dire*, of my own peculiar little fancies. I bear it with strange philosophy, but I do wish to be written to. I will tell you how I pass my time without society or exercise. Even till two o'clock, sometimes later, I pour ideas into the heads of the little Fullers; much runs out — indeed, I am often reminded of the chapter on home education, in the ' New Monthly.' But the few drops which remain mightily gladden the sight of my father. Then I go down-stairs and ask for my letters from the post; this is my only pleasure, according to the ideas most people entertain of pleasure. Do you write me an excellent epistle by return of mail, or I will make your head ache by a minute account of the way in which the remaining hours are spent. I have only lately read the 'Female Sovereigns' of your beloved Mrs. Jameson, and like them better than any of her works. Her opinions are clearly expressed, sufficiently discriminating, and her manner unusually simple. I was not dazzled by excess of artificial light, nor cloyed by spiced and sweetened sentiments. My love to your revered husband, and four kisses to Edward, two on your account, one for his beauty, and one abstract kiss, symbol of my love for all little children in general. Write of him, of Mr. ——'s sermons, of your likes and dislikes, of any new

characters, sublime or droll, you may have un-
earthed, and of all other things I should like.

"Affectionately your country friend, poor and
humble

"MARGARET."

In the summer of 1835 a great pleasure and
refreshment came to Margaret in the acquaintance of Miss Martineau, whom she met while
on a visit to her friend, Mrs. Farrar, in Cambridge. In speaking of this first meeting Margaret says: "I wished to give myself wholly
up to receive an impression of her. . . . What'
shrewdness in detecting various shades of character! Yet what she said of Hannah More
and Miss Edgeworth grated upon my feelings."
In a later conversation "the barrier that separates acquaintance from friendship" was passed,
and Margaret felt, beneath the sharpness of her
companion's criticism, the presence of a truly
human heart.

The two ladies went to church together, and
the minister prayed "for our friends." Margaret
was moved by this to offer a special prayer for
Miss Martineau, which so impressed itself upon
her mind that she was able to write it down.
We quote the part of it which most particularly
refers to her new friend : —

"May her path be guarded and blessed. May

her noble mind be kept firmly poised in its native truth, unsullied by prejudice or error, and strong to resist whatever outwardly or inwardly shall war against its high vocation. May each day bring to this generous seeker new riches of true philosophy and of Divine love. And, amidst all trials, give her to know and feel that thou, the All-sufficing, art with her, leading her on through eternity to likeness of thyself."

The change of base which, years after this time, transformed Miss Martineau into an enthusiastic disbeliever would certainly not have seemed to Margaret an answer to her prayer. But as the doctrine that "God reveals himself in many ways" was not new to her, and as her petition includes the Eternities, we may believe that she appreciated the sincerity of her friend's negations, and anticipated for her, as for herself, a later vision of the Celestial City, whose brightness should rise victorious above the mists of speculative doubt.

A serious illness intervened at this time, brought on, one might think, by the intense action of Margaret's brain, stimulated by her manifold and unremitting labors. For nine days and nights she suffered from fever, accompanied by agonizing pain in her head. Her beloved mother was at her bedside day and night. Her father, usually so reserved in expressions of affection, was moved by the near prospect of her death to say to her : " My dear, I have been thinking of you in the night, and I cannot remember that you have any *faults*. You have defects, of course, as all mortals have, but I do not know that you have a single fault." These words were intended by him as a *viaticum* for her, but they were really to be a legacy of love to his favorite child.

Margaret herself anticipated death with calmness, and, in view of the struggles and disappointments of life, with willingness. But the threatened bolt was to fall upon a head dearer to her than her own. In the early autumn of the same year her father, after a two days' illness, fell a victim to cholera.

Margaret's record of the grief which this affliction brought her is very deep and tender. Her father's image was ever present to her, and seemed even to follow her to her room, and to look in upon her there. Her most poignant sorrow was in the thought, suggested to many by similar afflictions, that she might have kept herself nearer to him in sympathy and in duty. The altered circumstances of the family, indeed, soon aroused her to new activities. Mr. Fuller had left no will, and had somewhat diminished his property by unproductive investments. Margaret now found new reason to wish that she

belonged to the sterner sex, since, had she
been eldest son instead of eldest daughter, she
might have become the administrator of her
father's estate and the guardian of her sister
and brothers. She regretted her ignorance of
such details of business as are involved in the
care of property, and determined to acquaint
herself with them, reflecting that "the same
mind which has made other attainments can in
time compass these." In this hour of trial she
seeks and finds relief and support in prayer.

"May God enable me to see the way clear,
and not to let down the intellectual in raising
the moral tone of my mind. Difficulties and
duties became distinct the very night after my
father's death, and a solemn prayer was offered
then that I might combine what is due to others
with what is due to myself. The spirit of that
prayer I shall constantly endeavor to maintain."

This death, besides the sorrow and perplexity
which followed it, brought to Margaret a disappointment which seemed to her to bar the fulfilment of her highest hopes. She had for two
years been contemplating a visit to Europe, with
a view to the better prosecution of her studies.
She had earned the right to this indulgence
beforehand, by assisting in the education of the
younger children of the family. An opportunity
now offered itself of making this journey under

the most auspicious circumstances. Her friends,
Mr. and Mrs. Farrar, were about to cross the
ocean, and had invited her to accompany them.
Miss Martineau was to be of the party, and Margaret now saw before her, not only this beloved
companionship, but also the open door which
would give her an easy access to literary society
in England, and to the atmosphere of old-world
culture which she so passionately longed to
breathe.

With this brilliant vision before her, and with
her whole literary future trembling, as she
thought, in the scale, Margaret prayed only
that she might make the right decision. This
soon became clear to her, and she determined,
in spite of the entreaties of her family, to remain
with her careworn mother, and not to risk the
possibility of encroaching upon the fund necessary for the education of her brothers and
sister.

Of all the crownings of Margaret's life, shall
we not most envy her that of this act of sacrifice ? So near to the feast of the gods, she prefers the fast of duty, and recognizes the claims
of family affection as more imperative than the
gratification of any personal taste or ambition.

Margaret does not seem to have been sup-
ported in this trial by any sense of its heroism.
Her decision was to her simply a following of

the right, in which she must be content, as she
says, to forget herself and act for the sake of
others.

We may all be glad to remember this example, and to refer to it those who find themselves
in a maze of doubt between what they owe to
the cultivation of their own gifts, what to the
need and advantage of those to whom they
stand in near relation. Had Margaret at this
time forsaken her darkened household, the difference to its members would have been very
great, and she herself would have added to the
number of those doubting or mistaken souls who
have been carried far from the scene of their
true and appointed service by some dream of
distinction never to be fulfilled. In the sequel
she was not only justified, but rewarded. The
sacrifice she had made secured the blessings of
education to the younger members of her family.
Her prayer that the lifting of her moral nature
might not lower the tone of her intellect was
answered, as it was sure to be, and she found
near at hand a field of honor and usefulness
which the brilliant capitals of Europe would
not have offered her.

Margaret's remaining days in Groton were
passed in assiduous reading, and her letters and
journals make suggestive comments on Goethe,

Shelley, Sir James Mackintosh, Herschel, Wordsworth, and others. Her scheme of culture was
what we should now call encyclopedic, and embraced most, if not all, departments of human
knowledge. If she was at all mistaken in her
scope, it was in this, that she did not sufficiently appreciate the inevitable limitations of
brain power and of bodily strength. Her impatience of such considerations led her to an
habitual over-use of her brilliant faculties which
resulted in an impaired state of health.

In the autumn of 1836 Margaret left Groton,
not without acknowledgment of " many precious
lessons given there in faith, fortitude, self-command, and unselfish love.

" There, too, in solitude, the mind acquired
more power of concentration, and discerned
the beauty of strict method ; there, too, more
than all, the heart was awakened to sympathize
with the ignorant, to pity the vulgar, to hope for
the seemingly worthless, and to commune with
the Divine Spirit of Creation."

CHAPTER V.

WINTER IN BOSTON. — A SEASON OF SEVERE LABOR.
— CONNECTION WITH GREENE STREET SCHOOL,
PROVIDENCE, R. I. — EDITORSHIP OF THE "DIAL."
— MARGARET'S ESTIMATE OF ALLSTON'S PICTURES.

MARGARET'S removal was to Boston, where a
twofold labor was before her. She was engaged
to teach Latin and French in Mr. Alcott's school,
then at the height of its prosperity, and intended
also to form classes of young ladies who should
study with her French, German, and Italian.

Mr. Alcott's educational theories did not altogether commend themselves to Margaret's judgment. They had in them, indeed, the germ of
much that is to-day recognized as true and important. But Margaret considered him to be
too much possessed with the idea of the unity
of knowledge, too little aware of the complexi-
ties of instruction.

He, on the other hand, describes her "as a person clearly given to the boldest speculation, and
of liberal and varied acquirements. Not wanting in imaginative power, she has the rarest
good sense and discretion. The blending of

sentiment and of wisdom in her is most remarkable, and her taste is as fine as her prudence. I think her the most brilliant talker of
her day."

Margaret now passed through twenty-five
weeks of incessant labor, suffering the while
from her head, which she calls "a bad head,"
but which we should consider a most abused
one. Her retrospect of this period of toil is
interesting, and with its severity she remembers also its value to her. Meeting with many
disappointments at the outset, and feeling pain-
fully the new circumstances which obliged her
to make merchandise of her gifts and acquirements, she yet says that she rejoices over it all,
"and would not have undertaken an iota less."
Besides fulfilling her intention of self-support,
she feels that she has gained in the power of
attention, in self-command, and in the knowledge of methods of instruction, without in the
least losing sight of the aims which had made
hitherto the happiness and enthusiasm of her
life.

Here is, in brief, the tale of her winter's work.

To one class she gave elementary instruction
in German, and that so efficiently that her pupils
were able to read the language with ease at the
end of three months. With another class she read,
in twenty-four weeks, Schiller's "Don Carlos,"

" Artists," and " Song of the Bell ; " Goethe's
" Herrman und Dorothea," " Götz von Berlich-
ingen," " Iphigenia," first part of " Faust," and
" Clavigo ; " Lessing's " Nathan der Weise,"
" Minna," and " Emilia Galotti ; " parts of
Tieck's " Phantasus," and nearly all of the first
volume of Richter's " Titan."

With the Italian class she read parts of Tasso,
Petrarch, Ariosto, Alfieri, and the whole hundred cantos of Dante's " Divina Commedia."
Besides these classes she had also three private
pupils, one of them a boy unable to use his eyes
in study. She gave this child oral instruction
in Latin, and read to him the History of England and Shakespeare's plays in connection.
The lessons given by her in Mr. Alcott's school
were, she says, valuable to her, but also very
fatiguing.

Though already so much overtasked, Margaret
found time and strength to devote one evening
every week to the *viva voce* translation of German authors for Dr. Channing's benefit, reading
to him mostly from De Wette and Herder.
Much conversation accompanied these readings,
and Margaret confesses that she finds therein
much food for thought, while the Doctor's judgments appear to her deliberate, and his sym-
pathies somewhat slow. She speaks of him as
entirely without any assumption of superiority

towards her, and as trusting " to the elevation of his thoughts to keep him in his place." She also greatly enjoyed his preaching, the force and earnestness of which seemed to her " to purge as by fire."

If Margaret was able to review her winter's work with pleasure, we must regard it with mingled wonder and dismay. The range and extent of her labors were indeed admirable, combining such extremes as enabled her to minister to the needs of the children in Mr. Alcott's school, and to assist the studies of the most eminent divine of the day. If we look only at her classes in literature, we shall find it wonderful that a woman of twenty-six should have been able to give available instruction in directions so many and various.

On the other hand, we must think that the immense extent of ground gone over involved too rapid a study of the separate works comprised in it. Here was given a synopsis of literary work which, properly performed, would fill a lifetime. It was no doubt valuable to her pupils through the vivifying influence of her enthusiastic imagination, which may have enabled some of them, in after years, to fill out the sketch of culture so boldly and broadly drawn before their eyes. Yet, considered as instruction, it must, from its very extent, have been somewhat superficial.

Our dismay would regard the remorseless degree in which Margaret, at this time, must have encroached upon the reserves of her bodily strength. Some physicists of to-day ascribe to women a peculiar power of concentrating upon one short effort an amount of vital force which should carry them through long years, and which, once expended, cannot be restored. Margaret's case would certainly justify this view ; for, while a mind so vigorous necessarily presupposes a body of uncommon vigor, she was after this time always a sufferer, and never enjoyed that perfect equipoise of function and of power which we call health.

In the spring of the year 1837 Margaret was invited to fill an important post in the Greene Street School, at Providence, R. I. It was proposed that she should teach the elder girls four hours daily, arranging studies and courses at her own discretion, and receiving a salary of one thousand dollars per annum.

Margaret hesitated to accept this offer, feeling inclined rather to renew her classes of the year just past, and having in mind also a life of Goethe which she greatly desired to write, and for which she was already collecting material. In the end, however, the prospect of immediate independence carried the day, and she

5

became the " Lady Superior," as she styles it, of the Providence school. Here a nearer view of the great need of her services stimulated her generous efforts, and she was rewarded by the love and reverence of her pupils, and by the knowledge that she did indeed bring them an awakening which led them from inert ignorance to earnest endeavor.

Margaret's record of her stay in Providence is enlivened by portraits of some of the men of mark who came within her ken. Among these was Tristam Burgess, already old, whose baldness, she says, " increases the fine effect of his appearance, for it seems as if the locks had re-treated that the contour of his strongly marked head might be revealed." The eminent lawyer, Whipple, is not, she says, a man of the Webster class ; but is, in her eyes, first among men of the class immediately below, and wears "a pervading air of ease and mastery which shows him fit to be a leader of the flock." John Neal, of Portland, speaks to her girls on the destiny and vocation of woman in America, and in private has a long talk with her concerning woman, whigism, modern English poets, Shakespeare, and particularly " Richard the Third," concerning which play the two " actually had a fight." " Mr. Neal," she says, " does not argue quite fairly, for he uses reason while it

lasts, and then helps himself out with wit, sentiment, and assertion." She hears a discourse and
prayer from Joseph John Gurney, of England,
in whose matter and manner she finds herself
grievously disappointed : " Quakerism has at
times looked lovely to me, and I had expected
at least a spiritual exposition of its doctrines
from the brother of Mrs. Fry. But his manner
was as wooden as his matter. His figures were
paltry, his thoughts narrowed down, and his
very sincerity made corrupt by spiritual pride.
The poet, Richard H. Dana, in those days gave
a course of readings from the English drama-
tists, beginning with Shakespeare. Margaret
writes : —

"The introductory was beautiful. . . . All
this was arrayed in a garb of most delicate
grace ; but a man of such genuine refinement
undervalues the cannon-blasts and rockets which
are needed to rouse the attention of the vulgar.
His naïve gestures, the rapt expression of his
face, his introverted eye, and the almost childlike
simplicity of his pathos carry one back into
a purer atmosphere, to live over again youth's
fresh emotions." Her *résumé* of him ends with
these words : "Mr. Dana has the charms and the
defects of one whose object in life has been to
preserve his individuality unprofaned."

Margaret's connection with the Greene Street

School in Providence lasted two years. Her success in this work was considered very great, and her brief residence in Rhode Island was crowned with public esteem and with many valued friendships.

Her parting from the pupils here was not without tears on both sides. Although engaged to teach the elder girls, Margaret's care had extended over the younger ones, and also over some of the boys. With all she exchanged an affectionate farewell, in which words of advice were mingled. To the class of girls which had been her especial charge she made a farewell address whose impressive sentences must have been long remembered. Here are some of them : —

"I reminded them of the ignorance in which some of them had been found, and showed them how all my efforts had necessarily been directed to stimulating their minds, leaving undone much which, under other circumstances, would have been deemed indispensable. I thanked them for the moral beauty of their conduct, bore witness that an appeal to conscience had never failed, and told them of my happiness in having the faith thus confirmed that young persons can be best guided by addressing their highest nature. I assured them of my true friendship, proved by my never having cajoled or caressed them into good. All my influence over them was rooted in reality; I had never softened nor palliated their faults. I had appealed, not to their weakness, but to their strength. I had offered to them always the loftiest motives, and had made every other end subservient to that of spiritual growth. With a heart-felt blessing I dismissed them."

In those days appeared Miss Martineau's book on America, of which we may say that its sharply critical tone stirred the national consciousness, and brought freshly into consideration the question of negro slavery, the discussion of which had been by common consent banished from " good " society in the United States. Miss Martineau dared to reprobate this institution in uncompromising language, and, while showing much appreciation of the natural beauties of the country, was generally thought to have done injustice to its moral and social characteristics.

While Margaret regarded with indignation the angry abuse with which her friend's book was greeted on this side of the Atlantic, she felt obliged to express to her the disappointment which she herself had felt on reading it. She acknowledges that the work has been " garbled, misrepresented, scandalously ill-treated." Yet she speaks of herself as one of those who, see-

ing in the book "a degree of presumptuousness,
irreverence, inaccuracy, hasty generalization, and
ultraism on many points which they did not
expect, lament the haste in which you have written, and the injustice which you have conse-
quently done to so important a task, and to your
own powers of being and doing."

Among other grievances, Margaret especially
felt the manner in which Miss Martineau had
written about Mr. Alcott. This she could not
pass over without comment : "A true and noble
man ; a philanthropist, whom a true and noble
woman, also a philanthropist, should have delighted to honor ; a philosopher, worthy the
palmy times of ancient Greece ; a man whom
the worldlings of Boston hold in as much horror
as the worldlings of ancient Athens did Socrates.
They smile to hear their verdict confirmed from
the other side of the Atlantic by their censor,
Harriet Martineau."

Margaret expresses in this letter the fear lest
the frankness of her strictures should deprive her
of the regard of her friend, but says, "If your
heart turns from me, I shall still love you, still
think you noble."

In 1840 Margaret was solicited to become the
editor of the "Dial," and undertook, for two
years, the management of the magazine, which

was at this time considered as the organ of the Transcendentalists. The "Dial" was a quarterly publication, somewhat nebulous in its character, but valuable as the expression of fresh thought, stimulating to culture of a new order. Like the transcendental movement itself, it had in it the germs of influences which in the course of the last forty years have come to be widely felt and greatly prized. In the newness of its birth and origin, it needed nursing fathers and nursing mothers, but was fed mostly, so far as concerns the general public, with neglect and ridicule.

Margaret, besides laboring with great diligence in her editorship, contributed to its pages many papers on her favorite points of study, such as Goethe, Beethoven, Romaic poetry, John Stirling, etc. Of the "Dial," Mr. Emerson says: "Good or bad, it cost a good deal of precious labor from those who served it, and from Margaret most of all." As there were no funds behind the enterprise, contributors were not paid for their work, and Margaret's modest salary of two hundred dollars per annum was discontinued after the first year.

The magazine lived four years. In England and Scotland it achieved a *succès d'estime*, and a republication of it in these days is about to make tardy amends for the general indifference which allowed its career to terminate so briefly.

Copies of the original work, now a literary curiosity, can here and there be borrowed from individuals who have grown old in the service of human progress. A look into the carefully preserved volumes shows us the changes which time has wrought in the four decades of years which have elapsed (quite or nearly) since the appearance of the last number.

A melancholy touches us as we glance hither and thither among its pages. How bright are the morning hours marked on this Dial! How merged now in the evening twilight and darkness! Here is Ralph Waldo Emerson, with life's meridian still before him. Here are printed some of his earliest lectures and some of the most admired of his poems. Here are the graceful verses of Christopher P. Cranch, artist and poet. Here are the Channing cousins, nephews of the great man by different brothers, one, William Henry Channing, then, as always, fervid and unrelinquishing in faith ; the other, William Ellery, a questioner who, not finding himself answered to his mind, has ceased to ask. Here is Theodore Parker, a youthful critic of existing methods and traditions, already familiar with the sacred writings of many religions. A. Bronson Alcott appears in various forms, contributing "Days from a Diary," "Orphic Sayings," and so on. Here are, from various authors, papers entitled: "Social Tendencies," "The Interior or Hidden Life," "The Pharisees," "Prophecy, Transcendentalism, and Progress," "Leaves from a Scholar's Journal," "Ethnic Scriptures," "The Preaching of Buddha," "Out-World and In-World," — headings which themselves afford an insight into the direction of the speculative thought and fancy of the time. An article on the Hollis Street Council presents to us the long-forgotten controversy between Rev. John Pierpont and his congregation, to settle which a conference of the Unitarian clergy was summoned. Another, entitled "Chardon Street and Bible Conventions," records the coming together of a company of "madmen, mad women, men with beards, Dunkers, Muggletonians, Come-outers, Groaners, Agrarians, Seventh-day Baptists, Quakers, Abolitionists, Calvinists, Unitarians, and Philosophers," to discuss church discipline and the authenticity of the Bible. Among those present were Dr. Channing, Father Taylor, Mr. Alcott, Mr. Garrison, Jones Very, and Mrs. Maria Weston Chapman. The chronicler says that "the assembly was characterized by the predominance of a certain plain, sylvan strength and earnestness, while many of the most intellectual and cultivated persons attended its councils. Mrs. Little and Mrs. Lucy Sessions took a pleasing and memorable part in the debate, and *that flea of Conventions,* Mrs. Abigail Folsom, was but too ready with her interminable scroll." In the July number of the year 1842 many pages are devoted to a rehearsal of " the entertainments of the past winter," which treats of Fanny Elssler's dancing, Braham's singing, oratorios, symphony concerts, and various lectures. Among these last, those of Mr. Lyell (afterwards Sir Charles) are curtly dismissed as " a neat article," while those of Henry Giles are recognized as showing popular talent.

Among Margaret's own contributions to the " Dial," the article on Goethe and that entitled " The Great Lawsuit" are perhaps the most noteworthy. We shall find the second of these expanded into the well-known "Woman in the Nineteenth Century," of which mention will be made hereafter. The one first named seems to demand some notice here, the fine discrimination of its criticism showing how well qualified the writer was to teach the women of her day the true appreciation of genius, and to warn them from the idolatry which worships the faults as well as the merits of great minds.

From a lover of Goethe, such sentences as the following were scarcely to have been expected : —

" Pardon him, World, that he was too worldly. Do not wonder, Heart, that he was so heartless.

Believe, Soul, that one so true, as far as he went, must yet be initiated into the deeper mysteries of soul.

"Naturally of a deep mind and shallow heart, he felt the sway of the affections enough to appreciate their working in other men, but never enough to receive their inmost regenerating influence."

Margaret finds a decline of sentiment and poetic power in Goethe, dating from his relinquishment of Lili.

"After this period we find in him rather a wide and deep wisdom than the inspirations of genius. His faith that all must issue well wants the sweetness of piety; and the God he manifests to us is one of law or necessity rather than of intelligent love.

"This mastery that Goethe prizes seems to consist rather in the skilful use of means than in the clear manifestation of ends. Yet never let him be confounded with those who sell all their birthright. He became blind to the more generous virtues, the nobler impulses, but ever in self-respect was busy to develop his nature. He was kind, industrious, wise, gentlemanly, if not manly."

Margaret, with bold and steady hand, draws a parallel between Dante's "Paradiso" and the second part of Goethe's "Faust." She prefers "the

grandly humble reliance of old Catholicism" to
" the loop-hole redemption of modern sagacity."
Yet she thinks that Dante, perhaps, " had not so
hard a battle to wage as this other great poet."
The fiercest passions she finds less dangerous to
the soul than the cold scepticism of the understanding. She sums up grandly the spiritual
ordeals of different historical periods : —

" The Jewish demon assailed the man of Uz
with physical ills, the Lucifer of the Middle Ages
tempted his passions ; but the Mephistopheles
of the eighteenth century bade the finite strive
to compass the infinite, and the intellect attempt
to solve all the problems of the soul."

Among Margaret's published papers on literature and art is one entitled " A Record of Impressions produced by the Exhibition of Mr.
Allston's Pictures in the Summer of 1839." She
was moved to write this, she says, partly by the
general silence of the press on a matter of so
much import in the history of American art, and
partly by the desire to analyze her own views,
and to ascertain, if possible, the reason why, at
the close of the exhibition, she found herself less
a gainer by it than she had expected. As Margaret gave much time and thought to art matters, and as the Allston exhibition was really an
event of historic interest, some consideration

of this paper will not be inappropriate in this place.

Washington Allston was at that time, had long been, and long continued to be, the artist saint of Boston. A great personal prestige added its power to that of his unquestioned genius.

Beautiful in appearance, as much a poet as a painter, he really seemed to belong to an order of beings who might be called

> "Too bright and good
> For human nature's daily food."

He had flown into the heart of Europe when few American artists managed to get so far. He had returned to live alone with his dreams, of which one was the nightmare of a great painting which he never could finish, and never did. He had kept the vulgar world at a distance from his life and thought, intent on coining these into a succession of pictures which claimed to have a mission to the age. The series of female heads which are the most admirable of his works appeared to be the portraits of as many ideal women who, with no existence elsewhere, had disclosed themselves to him at his dreamy fireside or in his haunted studio. The spirit of the age, in its highest extreme, was upon him, and the wave of supervital aspiration swept him, as it did

Channing and Emerson, beyond the region of the visible and sensible. At that day, and for ten years later, one might occasionally have seen in some street of Boston a fragile figure, and upon it a head distinguished by snowy curls and starry eyes. Here was the winter of age; here the perpetual summer of the soul. The coat and hat did not matter; but they were of some quaint, forgotten fashion, outlining the vision as belonging to the past. You felt a modesty in looking at anything so unique and delicate. I remember this vision as suddenly disclosed out of a bitter winter's day. And the street was Chestnut Street, and the figure was Washington Allston going to visit the poet Richard H. Dana. And not long afterwards the silvery snows melted, and the soul which had made those eyes so luminous shot back to its immortal sphere.

But, to leave the man and return to the artist. Mr. Allston's real merit was too great to be seriously obscured by the over-sweep of imagination to which he was subject. His best works still remain true classics of the canvas; but the spirit which, through them, seemed to pass from his mind into that of the public, has not to-day the recognition and commanding interest which it then had.

Margaret had expected, as she says, to be

greatly a gainer by her study of this exhibition, and had been somewhat disappointed. Possibly her expectations regarded a result too immediate and definite. Sights and experiences that enrich the mind often do so insensibly. They pass out of our consciousness ; but in our later judgments we find our standard changed, and refer back to them as the source of its enlargement.

Margaret was already familiar with several of the ideal heads of which we have spoken, and which bore the names of Beatrice, Rosalie, the Valentine, etc. Of these, as previously seen and studied, she says : —

"The calm and meditative cast of these pictures, the ideal beauty that shone through rather than in them, and the harmony of coloring were as unlike anything else I saw, as the 'Vicar of Wakefield' to Cooper's novels. I seemed to recognize in painting that self-possessed elegance, that transparent depth, which I most admire in literature."

With these old favorites she classes, as most beautiful among those now shown, the Evening Hymn, the Italian Shepherd Boy, Edwin, Lorenzo and Jessica.

" The excellence of these pictures is subjective, and even feminine. They tell us the painter's ideal of character : a graceful repose, with a fitness for moderate action ; a capacity

of emotion, with a habit of reverie. Not one
of these beings is in a state of *épanchement*.
Not one is, or perhaps could be, thrown off its
equipoise. They are, even the softest, characterized by entire though unconscious self-possession."

The head called Beatrice was sometimes
spoken of in those days as representing the
Beatrice of Dante. Margaret finds in it nothing
to suggest the " Divina Commedia."

" How fair, indeed, and not unmeet for a poet's
love. But what she is, what she can be, it
needs no Dante to discover. She is not a lus-
trous, bewitching beauty, neither is she a high
and poetic one. She is not a concentrated per-
fume, nor a flower, nor a star. Yet somewhat
has she of every creature's best. She has the
golden mean, without any touch of the medi-
ocre."

The landscapes in the exhibition gave her
"unalloyed delight." She found in them Mr.
Allston's true mastery,—"a power of sympathy,
which gives each landscape a perfectly individual character. . . . The soul of the painter,"
she says, "is in these landscapes, but not his
character. Is not that the highest art ? Nature
and the soul combined ; the former freed from
crudities or blemishes, the latter from its merely
human aspect."

Allston's Miriam suggests to Margaret a different treatment of the subject: —

" This maiden had been nurtured in a fair and highly civilized country, in the midst of wrong and scorn indeed, but beneath the shadow of sublime institutions. Amid all the pains and penances of slavery, the memory of Joseph, the presence of Moses, exalt her soul to the highest pitch of national pride.

" Imagine the stately and solemn beauty with which such nurture and such a position might invest the Jewish Miriam. Imagine her at the moment when her lips were unsealed, and she was permitted to sing the song of deliverance. Realize this situation, and oh, how far will this beautiful picture fall short of your demands ! "

To such a criticism Mr. Allston might have replied that a picture in words is one thing, a picture in colors quite another; and that the complex intellectual expression in which Margaret delighted is appropriate to literary, but not to pictorial art.

Much in the same way does she reason concerning one of Allston's most admired paintings, which represents Jeremiah in prison dictating to Baruch : —

" The form of the prophet is brought out in such noble relief, is in such fine contrast to the pale and feminine sweetness of the scribe at his

6

feet, that for a time you are satisfied. But by
and by you begin to doubt whether this picture
is not rather imposing than majestic. The dignity of the prophet's appearance seems to lie
rather in the fine lines of the form and drapery
than in the expression of the face. It was well
observed by one who looked on him, that, if the
eyes were cast down, he would become an ordinary man. This is true, and the expression of
the bard must not depend on a look or gesture,
but beam with mild electricity from every feature. Allston's Jeremiah is not the mournfully
indignant bard, but the robust and stately Jew,
angry that men will not mark his word and go
his way."

The test here imagined, that of concealing
the eyes, would answer as little in real as in
pictured life. Although the method of these
criticisms is arbitrary, the conclusion to which
they bring Margaret is one in which many will
agree with her : —

"The more I have looked at these pictures,
the more I have been satisfied that the grand
historical style did not afford the scope most
proper to Mr. Allston's genius. The Prophets
and Sibyls are for the Michael Angelos. The
Beautiful is Mr. Allston's dominion. Here he
rules as a genius, but in attempts such as I have
been considering, can only show his apprecia-

tion of the stern and sublime thoughts he wants force to reproduce."

Margaret is glad to go back from these more labored and unequal compositions to those lovely feminine creations which had made themselves so beloved that they seemed to belong to the spiritual family of Boston itself, and to " have floated across the painter's heaven on the golden clouds of fantasy."

From this paper our thoughts naturally revert to what Mr. Emerson has said of Margaret as an art critic : —

" Margaret's love of art, like that of most cultivated persons in this country, was not at all technical, but truly a sympathy with the artist in the protest which his work pronounced on the deformity of our daily manners ; her co-perception with him of the eloquence of form ; her aspiration with him to a fairer life. As soon as her conversation ran into the mysteries of manipulation and artistic effect, it was less trustworthy. I remember that in the first times when I chanced to see pictures with her, I listened reverently to her opinions, and endeavored to see what she saw. But on several occasions, finding myself unable to reach it, I came to suspect my guide, and to believe at last that her taste in works of art, though honest, was not on universal, but on idiosyncratic grounds."

CHAPTER VI.

WILLIAM HENRY CHANNING'S PORTRAIT OF MAR-
GARET. — TRANSCENDENTAL DAYS. — BROOK
FARM. — MARGARET'S VISITS THERE.

IT iş now time for us to speak of the portrait of
Margaret drawn by the hand of William Henry
Channing. And first give us leave to say that
Mr. Emerson's very valuable statements concerning her are to be prized rather for their
critical and literary appreciation than accepted
as showing the insight given by strong personal
sympathy.

While bound to each other by mutual esteem
and admiration, Margaret and Mr. Emerson
were opposites in natural tendency, if not in
character. While Mr. Emerson never appeared
to be modified by any change of circumstance,
never melted nor took fire, but was always and
everywhere himself, the soul of Margaret was
subject to a glowing passion which raised the
temperature of the social atmosphere around
her. Was this atmosphere heavy with human
dulness ? Margaret so smote the ponderous
demon with her fiery wand that he was presently

compelled to " caper nimbly " for her amusement, or to flee from her presence. Was sorrow master of the situation ? Of this tyranny Margaret was equally intolerant. The mourner must be uplifted through her to new hope and joy. Frivolity and all unworthiness had reason to fear her, for she denounced them to the face, with somnambulic unconcern. But where high joys were in the ascendant, there stood Margaret, quick with her inner interpretation, adding to human rapture itself the deep, calm lessoning of divine reason. A priestess of life-glories, she magnified her office, and in its grandeur sometimes grew grandiloquent. But with all this her sense was solid, and her meaning clear and worthy.

Mr. Emerson had also a priesthood, but of a different order. The calm, severe judgment, the unpardoning taste, the deliberation which not only preceded but also followed his utterances, carried him to a remoteness from the common life of common people, and allowed no intermingling of this life with his own. For him, too, came a time of fusion which vindicated his interest in the great issues of his time. But this was not in Margaret's day, and to her he seemed the palm-tree in the desert, graceful and admirable, bearing aloft a waving crest, but spreading no sheltering and embracing branches.

William Henry Channing, whose reminiscences of Margaret stand last in order in the
memoirs already published, was more nearly
allied to her in character than either of his
coadjutors. If Mr. Emerson's bane was a want
of fusion, the ruling characteristic of Mr. Channing was a heart that melted almost too easily
at the touch of human sympathy, and whose
heat and glow of feeling may sometimes have
overswept the calmer power of judgment.

He had heard of Margaret in her school-girl
days as a prodigy of talent and attainment.
During the period of his own studies in Cambridge he first made her acquaintance. He
was struck, but not attracted, by her " saucy
sprightliness." Her intensity of temperament,
unmeasured satire, and commanding air were
indeed somewhat repellent to him, and almost
led him to conjecture that she had chosen for her
part in life the *rôle* of a Yankee Corinne. Her
friendships, too, seemed to him extravagant. He
dreaded the encounter of a personality so impe-
rious and uncompromising in its demands, and
was content to observe her at a safe and respectful distance. Soon, however, through the
"shining fog" of brilliant wit and sentiment
the real nobility of her nature made itself seen
and felt. He found her sagacious in her judgments. Her conversation showed breadth of

culture and depth of thought. Above all, he was made to feel her great sincerity of purpose. " This it was," says he, " that made her criticism so trenchant, her contempt of pretence so quick and stern." The loftiness of her ideal explained the severity of her judgments, and the heroic mould and impulse of her character had much to do with her stately deportment. Thus the salient points which, at a distance, had seemed to him defects, were found, on a nearer view, to be the indications of qualities most rare and admirable.

James Freeman Clarke, an intimate of both parties, made them better known to each other by his cordial interpretation of each to each. But it was in the year 1839, in the days of Margaret's residence at Jamaica Plain, that the friendship between these two eminent persons, " long before rooted, grew up, and leafed, and blossomed." Mr. Channing traces the beginning of this nearer relation to a certain day on which he sought Margaret amid these new surroundings. It was a bright summer day. The windows of Margaret's parlor commanded a pleasant view of meadows, with hills beyond. She entered, bearing a vase of freshly gathered flowers, her own tribute just levied from the garden. Of these, and of their significance, was her first speech. From these she passed to the engravings which adorned her walls, and to much talk of art and artists. From this theme an easy transition led the conversation to Greece and its mythology. A little later, Margaret began to speak of the friends whose care had surrounded her with these objects of her delighting contemplation. The intended marriage of two of the best beloved among these friends was much in her mind at the moment, and Mr. Channing compares the gradation of thought by which she arrived at the announcement of this piece of intelligence to the progress and *dénouement* of a drama, so eloquent and artistic did it appear to him.

A ramble in Bussey's woods followed this indoor interview. In his account of it Mr. Channing has given us not only a record of much that Margaret said, but also a picture of how she looked on that ever-remembered day.

"Reaching a moss-cushioned ledge near the summit, she seated herself. . . . As, leaning on one arm, she poured out her stream of thought, turning now and then her eyes full upon me, to see whether I caught her meaning, there was leisure to study her thoroughly. Her temperament was predominantly what the physiologists would call nervous-sanguine ; and the gray eye, rich brown hair, and light complexion, with the muscular and well-developed frame, bespoke delicacy balanced by vigor. Here was a sensitive yet powerful being, fit at once for rapture or sustained effort. She certainly had not beauty ; yet the high-arched dome of the head, the changeful expressiveness of every feature, and her whole air of mingled dignity and impulse gave her a commanding charm."

Mr. Channing mentions, as others do, Margaret's habit of shutting her eyes, and opening them suddenly, with a singular dilatation of the iris. He dwells still more upon the pliancy of her neck, the expression of which varied with her mood of mind. In moments of tender or pensive feeling its curves were like those of a swan ; under the influence of indignation its movements were more like the swoopings of a bird of prey.

"Finally, in the animation yet *abandon* of Margaret's attitude and look were rarely blended the fiery force of Northern, and the soft languor of Southern races."

Until this day Mr. Channing had known Margaret through her intellect only. This conversation of many hours revealed her to him in a new light. It unfolded to him her manifold gifts and her deep experience, her great capacity for joy, and the suffering through which she had passed. She should have been an acknowledged queen among the magnates of European culture : she was hedged about by the narrow intolerance of provincial New England.

In a more generous soil her genius would
have borne fruit of the highest order. She felt
this, felt that she failed of this highest result,
and was yet so patient, so faithful to duty, so
considerate of all who had claims upon her!
Perceiving now the ardor of her nature and the
strength of her self-sacrifice, Margaret's new
friend could not but bow in reverence before
her; and from that time the two always met as
intimates.

Mr. Channing's reminiscences preserve for us
a valuable *aperçu* of the Transcendental movement in New England, and of Margaret's relation to it.

The circle of the Transcendentalists was, for
the moment, a new church, with the joy and
pain of a new evangel in its midst. In the very
heart of New England Puritanism, at that day
hard, dry, and thorny, had sprung up a new
growth, like the blossoming of a century-plant,
beautiful and inconvenient. Boundaries had to
be enlarged for it; for if society would not give
it room, it was determined to go outside of society, and to assert, at all hazards, the freedom
of inspiration.

While this movement was in a good degree
one of simple protest and reaction, it yet drew
much of its inspiration from foreign countries
and periods of time remote from our own.

From the standpoint of the present it looked deeply into the past and into the future. Its leaders studied Plato, Seneca, Epictetus, Plutarch, among the classic authors, and De Wette, Hegel, Kant, and Fichte, among the prophets of modern thought. The *welt-geist* of the Germans was its ideal. Method, it could not boast. Free discussion, abstinence from participation in ordinary social life and religious worship, a restless seeking for sympathy, and a constant formulation of sentiments which, exalted in themselves, seemed to lose something of their character by the frequency with which they were presented, — these are some of the traits which Transcendentalism showed to the uninitiated.

To its Greek and Germanic elements was presently added an influence borrowed from the systematic genius of France. The works of Fourier became a gospel of hope to those who looked for a speedy regeneration of society. George Ripley, an eminent scholar and critic, determined to embody this hope in a grand experiment, and bravely organized the Brook Farm Community upon a plan as nearly in accordance with the principles laid down by Fourier as circumstances would allow. He was accompanied in this new departure by a little band of fellow-workers, of whom one or two were already well known as literary men, while others of them have since attained distinction in various walks of life.

While all the Transcendentalists were not associationists, the family at Brook Farm was yet considered as an outcome of the new movement, and as such was regarded by its promoters with great sympathy and interest.

Margaret's position among the Transcendentalists may easily be imagined. In such a group of awakened thinkers her place was soon determined. At their frequent reunions she was a most welcome and honored guest. More than this. Among those who claimed a fresh outpouring of the Spirit Margaret was recognized as a bearer of the living word. She was not in haste to speak on these occasions, but seemed for a time absorbed in listening and in observation. When the moment came, she showed the results of this attention by briefly restating the points already touched upon, passing thence to the unfolding of her own views. This she seems always to have done with much force, and with a grace no less remarkable. She spoke slowly at first, with the deliberation inseparable from weight of thought. As she proceeded, images and illustrations suggested themselves to her mind in rapid succession. "The sweep of her speech became grand," says Mr. Channing. Her eloquence was direct and vigorous. Her wide range of reading supplied her with ready and copious illustrations. The commonplace be-

came original from her way of treating it. She
had power to analyze, power to sum up. Her
use of language had a rhythmic charm. She was
sometimes grandiloquent, sometimes excessive in
her denunciation of popular evils and abuses, but
her sincerity of purpose, her grasp of thought and
keenness of apprehension, were felt throughout.

The source of these and similar sibylline mani-
festations is a subtle one. Such a speaker,
consciously or unconsciously, draws much of her
inspiration from the minds of those around her.
Each of these in a measure affects her, while she
still remains mistress of herself. Her thought
is upheld by the general sympathy, which she
suddenly lifts to a height undreamed of before.
She divines what each most purely wishes, most
deeply hopes ; and so her words reveal to those
present not only their own unuttered thoughts,
but also the higher significance and completeness which she is able to give to these thoughts
under the seal of her own conviction. These
fleeting utterances, alas ! are lost, like the leaves
swept of old from the sibyl's cave. But as souls
are, after all, the most permanent facts that we
know of, who shall say that one breath of them
is wasted ?

Young hearts to-day, separated from the time
we speak of by two or three generations, may

still keep the generous thrill which Margaret awakened in the bosom of a grandmother, herself then in the bloom of youth. Books, indeed, are laid away and forgotten, manuscripts are lost or destroyed. The spoken word, fleeting though it be, may kindle a flame that ages shall not quench, but only brighten.

While, therefore, it may well grieve us to-day that we cannot know exactly what Margaret said nor how she said it, we may believe that the inspiration which she felt and communicated to others remains, not the less, a permanent value in the community.

Having already somewhat the position of a "come-outer," Margaret was naturally supposed to be in entire sympathy with the Transcendentalists. This supposition was strengthened by her assuming the editorship of the "Dial," and Christopher Cranch, in caricaturing it, represented her as a Minerva driving a team of the new *illuminati*. Margaret's journals and letters, however, show that while she welcomed the new outlook towards a possible perfection, she did not accept without reserve the enthusiasms of those about her. "The good time coming," which seemed to them so near, appeared to her very distant, and difficult of attainment. Her views at the outset are aptly expressed in the following extract from one of her letters: —

"Utopia it is impossible to build up   At least, my hopes for our race on this one planet are more limited than those of most of my friends.   I accept the limitations of human nature, and believe a wise acknowledgment of them one of the best conditions of progress. Yet every noble scheme, every poetic manifestation, prophesies to man his eventual destiny. And were not man ever more sanguine than facts at the moment justify, he would remain torpid, or be sunk in sensuality.   It is on this ground that I sympathize with what is called the 'Transcendental party,' and that I feel their aim to be the true one."

The grievance maintained against society by the new school of thought was of a nature to make the respondent say: "We have piped unto you, and ye have not danced; we have mourned unto you, and ye have not wept." The status of New England, social and political, was founded upon liberal traditions.   Yet these friends placed themselves in opposition to the whole existing order of things.   The Unitarian discipline had delivered them from the yoke of doctrines impossible to an age of critical culture. They reproached it with having taken away the mystical ideas which, in imaginative minds, had made the poetry of the old faith.   Margaret, writing of these things in 1840, well says:

"Since the Revolution there has been little in the circumstances of this country to call out the higher sentiments. The effect of continued prosperity is the same on nations as on individuals; it leaves the nobler faculties undeveloped. The superficial diffusion of knowledge, unless attended by a deepening of its sources, is likely to vulgarize rather than to raise the thought of a nation. . . . The tendency of circumstances has been to make our people superficial, irreverent, and more anxious to get a living than to live mentally and morally." So much for the careless crowd. In another sentence, Margaret gives us the clew to much of the "divine discontent" felt by deeper thinkers. She says : "How much those of us who have been formed by the European mind have to unlearn and lay aside, if we would act here ! "

The scholars of New England had indeed so devoted themselves to the study of foreign literatures as to be little familiar with the spirit and the needs of their own country. The England of the English classics, the Germany of the German poets and philosophers, the Italy of the Renaissance writers and artists, combined to make the continent in which their thoughts were at home. The England of the commonalty, the Germany and Italy of the peasant and artisan, were little known to them, and as little the characteristic qualities and defects of their own country-people. Hence their comparison of the old society with the new was in great part founded upon what we may call "literary illusions." Moreover, the German and English methods of thought were only partially applicable to a mode of life whose conditions far transcended those of European life in their freedom and in the objects recognized as common to all.

Those of us who have numbered threescore years can remember the perpetual lamentation of the cultivated American of forty years ago. His whole talk was a cataloguing of negatives : "We have not this, we have not that." To all of which the true answer would have been: "You have a wonderful country, an exceptional race, an unparalleled opportunity. You have not yet made your five talents ten. That is what you should set about immediately."

The Brook Farm experiment probably appeared to Margaret in the light of an Utopia. Her regard for the founders of the enterprise induced her, nevertheless, to visit the place frequently. Of the first of these visits her journal has preserved a full account.

The aspect of the new settlement at first appeared to her somewhat desolate : "You seem to belong to nobody, to have a right to speak to nobody ; but very soon you learn to take care of

7

yourself, and then the freedom of the place is delightful."

The society of Mr. and Mrs. Ripley was most congenial to her, and the nearness of the woods afforded an opportunity for the rambles in which she delighted. But her time was not all dedicated to these calm pleasures. Soon she had won the confidence of several of the inmates of the place, who imparted to her their heart histories, seeking that aid and counsel which she was so well able to give. She mentions the holding of two conversations during this visit, in both of which she was the leader. The first was on Education, a subject concerning which her ideas differed from those adopted by the Community. The manners of some of those present were too free and easy to be agreeable to Margaret, who was accustomed to deference.

At the second conversation, some days later, the circle was smaller, and no one showed any sign of weariness or indifference. The subject was Impulse, chosen by Margaret because she observed among her new friends "a great tendency to advocate spontaneousness at the expense of reflection." Of her own part in this exercise she says : —

"I defended nature, as I always do, — the spirit ascending through, not superseding nature. But in the scale of sense, intellect, spirit, I advo-

cated to-night the claims of intellect, because
those present were rather disposed to postpone
them."

After the lapse of a year she found the tone
of the society much improved. The mere freak-
ishness of unrestraint had yielded to a recognition of the true conditions of liberty, and
tolerance was combined with sincerity.

CHAPTER VII.

AMONG Margaret's life-long characteristics was
a genuine love of little children, which sprang
from a deep sense of the beauty and sacredness
of childhood. When she visited the homes of
her friends, the little ones of their households
were taken into the circle of her loving attention.
Three of these became so especially dear to her
that she called them her children. These were
Waldo Emerson, Pickie Greeley, and Herman
Clarke. For each of them the span of earthly
life was short, no one of them living to pass out
of childhood.

Waldo was the eldest son of Mr. Emerson,
the child deeply mourned and commemorated
by him in the well-known threnody : —

" The hyacinthine boy for whom
　　Morn well might break and April bloom.
　The gracious boy who did adorn
　　The world whereinto he was born,

And by his countenance repay
The favor of the loving Day,
Has disappeared from the Day's eye.

This death occurred in 1841. Margaret visited
Concord soon afterward, and has left in her journals a brief record of this visit, in which she
made the grief of her friends her own. We
gather from its first phrase that Mr. Emerson,
whom she now speaks of as "Waldo," had wished
her to commit to writing some of her reminiscences of the dear one lately departed : —

"Waldo brought me at once the inkhorn and
pen. I told him if he kept me so strictly to
my promise I might lose my ardor ; however,
I began at once to write for him, but not with
much success. Lidian came in to see me before
dinner. She wept for the lost child, and I was
tempted to do the same, which relieved much
from the oppression I have felt since. I came.
Waldo showed me all he and others had written
about the child ; there is very little from Waldo's
own observation, though he was with him so
much. He has not much eye for the little signs
in children that have such great leadings. The
little there is, is good.

"'Mamma, may I have this little bell which
I have been making, to stand by the side of my
bed?'

"'Yes, it may stand there.'

" 'But, mamma, I am afraid it will alarm you. It may sound in the middle of the night, and it will be heard over the whole town. It will sound like some great glass thing which will fall down and break all to pieces ; it will be louder than a thousand hawks ; it will be heard across the water and in all the countries, it will be heard all over the world.'

" I like this, because it was exactly so he talked, spinning away without end and with large, beautiful, earnest eyes. But most of the stories are of short sayings.

" This is good in M. Russell's journal of him. She had been telling him a story that excited him, and then he told her this : ' How his horse went out into a long, long wood, and how he looked through a squirrel's eyes and saw a great giant, and the giant was himself.'

. . . .

" Went to see the Hawthornes ; it was very pleasant, the poplars whisper so suddenly their pleasant tale, and everywhere the view is so peaceful. The house within I like, all their things are so expressive of themselves and mix in so gracefully with the old furniture. H. walked home with me ; we stopped some time to look at the moon. She was struggling with clouds. He said he should be much more willing to die than two months ago, for he had had some real possession in life ; but still he never wished to leave this earth, it was beautiful enough. He expressed, as he always does, many fine perceptions. I like to hear the lightest thing he says.

"Waldo and I have good meetings, though we stop at all our old places. But my expectations are moderate now ; it is his beautiful presence that I prize far more than our intercourse. He has been reading me his new poems, and the other day at the end he asked me how I liked the 'little subjective twinkle all through.'

. . . .

Saturday. Dear Richard has been here a day or two, and his common sense and homely affection are grateful after these fine people with whom I live at sword's points, though for the present turned downwards. It is well to 'thee' and 'thou' it after talking with angels and geniuses. Richard and I spent the afternoon at Walden and got a great bunch of flowers. A fine thunder-shower gloomed gradually up and turned the lake inky black, but no rain came till sunset.

"*Sunday.* A heavy rain. I must stay at home. I feel sad. Mrs. Ripley was here, but I only saw her a while in the afternoon and spent the day in my room. Sunday I do not give to my duty writing, no indeed. I finished yesterday, after a rest, the article on ballads. Though a patchwork thing, it has craved time to do it."

We come now to the period of the famous conversations in which, more fully than in aught else, Margaret may be said to have delivered her message to the women of her time. The novelty of such a departure in the Boston of forty years ago may be imagined, and also the division of opinion concerning it in those social circles which consider themselves as charged with the guardianship of the taste of the community. Margaret's attitude in view of this undertaking appears to have been a modest and sensible one. She found herself, in the first place, under the necessity of earning money for her own support and in aid of her family. Her greatest gift, as she well knew, was in conversation. Her rare eloquence did not much avail her at her desk, and though all that she wrote had the value of thought and of study, it was in living speech alone that her genius made itself entirely felt and appreciated. What more natural than that she should have proposed to make this rare gift available for herself and others? The reasons which she herself gives for undertaking the experiment are so solid and sufficient as to make us blush retrospectively for the merriment in which the thoughtless world sometimes indulged concerning her. Her wish was "to pass in review the departments of thought and knowledge, and endeavor to place them in due relation to one another in our minds ; to systematize thought, and give a precision and clearness in which our sex are so deficient, chiefly, I think, because they have so few inducements to test and classify what they receive." In fine, she hoped to be able to throw some light upon the momentous questions, " What were we born to do, and how shall we do it ? "

In looking forward to this effort, she saw one possible obstacle in "that sort of vanity which wears the garb of modesty," and which, she thinks, may make some women fear "to lay aside the shelter of vague generalities, the art of coterie criticism," and the "delicate disdains of *good society,*" even to obtain a nearer view of truth itself. "Yet," she says, "as without such generous courage nothing of value can be learned or done, I hope to see many capable of it."

The twofold impression which Margaret made is to be remarked in this matter of the conversations, as elsewhere. Without the fold of her admirers stood carping, unkind critics ; within were enthusiastic and grateful friends.

The first meeting of Margaret's Conversation Class was held at Miss Peabody's rooms, in West Street, Boston, on the 6th of November, 1839.

Twenty-five ladies were present, who showed themselves to be of the elect by their own election of a noble **aim**. These were all ladies of superior position, gathered by a common interest from very various belongings of creed and persuasion. At this, their first coming together, Margaret prefaced her programme by some remarks on the deficiencies in the education given to women, defects which she thought that later study, aided by the stimulus of mutual endeavor and interchange of thought, might do much to remedy. Her opening remarks are as instructive to-day as they were when she uttered them : —

"Women are now taught, at school, all that men are. They run over, superficially, even *more* studies, without being really taught anything. But with this difference : men are called on, from a very early period, to reproduce all that they learn. Their college exercises, their political duties, their professional studies, the first actions of life in any direction, call on them to put to use what they have learned. But women learn without any attempt to reproduce. Their only reproduction is for purposes of display. It is to supply this defect that these conversations have been planned."

Margaret had chosen the Greek Mythology for the subject of her first conversations. Her reasons for this selection are worth remembering : —

"It is quite separated from all exciting local subjects. It is serious without being solemn, and without excluding any mode of intellectual action; it is playful as well as deep. It is sufficiently wide, for it is a complete expression of the cultivation of a nation. It is also generally known, and associated with all our ideas of the arts."

In considering this statement it is not difficult for us at this day to read, as people say, between the lines. The religious world of Margaret's youth was agitated by oppositions which rent asunder the heart of Christendom. Margaret wished to lead her pupils beyond all discord, into the high and happy unity. Her own nature was both fervent and religious, but she could not accept intolerance either in belief or in disbelief. To study with her friends the ethics of an ancient faith, too remote to become the occasion of personal excitement, seemed to her a step in the direction of freer thought and a more unbiassed criticism. The Greek mythology, instinct with the genius of a wonderful people, afforded her the desired theme. With its help she would introduce her pupils to a sphere of serenest contemplation, in which Religion and Beauty had become wedded through immortal types.

Margaret was not able to do this without

awakening some orthodox suspicion. This she knew how to allay; for when one of the class demurred at the supposition that a Christian nation could have anything to envy in the religion of a heathen one, Margaret said that she had no desire to go back, and believed we have the elements of a deeper civilization; yet the Christian was in its infancy, the Greek in its maturity, nor could she look on the expression of a great nation's intellect as insignificant. These fables of the gods were the result of the universal sentiments of religion, aspiration, intellectual action, of a people whose political and æsthetic life had become immortal.

Margaret's good hopes were justified by the success of her undertaking. The value of what she had to impart was felt by her class from the first. It was not received in a passive and compliant manner, but with the earnest questioning which she had wished to awaken, and which she was so well able both to promote and to satisfy.

In the first of her conversations ten of the twenty-five persons present took part, and this number continued to increase in later meetings. Some of these ladies had been bred in the ways of liberal thought, some held fast to the formal limits of the old theology. The extremes of bigotry and scepticism were probably not unrep-

resented among them. From these differences
and dissidences Margaret was able to combine
the elements of a wider agreement. A common
ground of interest was found in the range of
topics presented by her, and in her manner of
presenting them. The enlargement of a new
sympathy was made to modify the intense and
narrow interests in which women, as a class, are
apt to abide.

Margaret's journal and letters to friends give
some accounts of the first meetings. She finds
her circle, from the start, devoutly thoughtful,
and feels herself, not "a paid Corinne," but a
teacher and a guide. The bright minds respond
to her appeal, as half-kindled coals glow beneath
a strong and sudden breath. The present, always arid if exclusively dwelt in, is enriched by
the treasures of the past and animated by the
great hopes of the future.

Reports from some of Margaret's hearers show
us how she appeared to them : —

"All was said with the most captivating address and grace, and with beautiful modesty.
The position in which she placed herself with
respect to the rest was entirely lady-like and
companionable."

Another writer finds in the *séance* " the charm
of a Platonic dialogue," without pretension or
pedantry. Margaret, in her chair of leadership,

appeared positively beautiful in her intelligent enthusiasm. Even her dress was glorified by this influence, and is spoken of as sumptuous, although it is known to have been characterized by no display or attempted effect.

In Margaret's plan the personages of the Greek Olympus were considered as types of various aspects of human character. Prometheus became the embodiment of pure reason. Jupiter stood for active, Juno for passive will, the one representing insistence, the other resistance. Minerva pictured the practical power of the intellect. Apollo became the symbol of genius, Bacchus that of geniality. Venus was instinctive womanhood, and also a type of the Beautiful, to the consideration of which four conversations were devoted. In a fifth, Margaret related the story of Cupid and Psyche in a manner which indelibly impressed itself upon the minds of her hearers. Other conversations presented Neptune as circumstance, Pluto as the abyss of the undeveloped, Pan as the glow and play of nature, etc. Thus in picturesque guise the great questions of life and of character were passed in review. A fresh and fearless analysis of human conditions showed, as a discovery, the grandeur and beauty of man's spiritual inheritance. All were cheered and uplifted by this new outlook, sharing for the time and perhaps thenceforth what Mr. Emerson calls " the steady elevation of Margaret's aim."

These occasions, so highly prized and enjoyed, sometimes brought to Margaret their penalty in the shape of severe nervous headache. During one of these attacks a friend expressed anxiety lest she should continue to suffer in this way. Margaret replied : " I feel just now such a separation from pain and illness, such a consciousness of true life while suffering most, that pain has no effect but to steal some of my time."

In accordance with the urgent desire of the class the conversations were renewed at the beginning of the following winter, Margaret having in the mean time profited by a season of especial retirement which was not without influence upon her plan of thought and of life. From this interval of religious contemplation she returned to her labors with the feeling of a new power. In opening the first meeting of this second series, on November 22, 1840, Margaret spoke of great changes which had taken place in her way of thinking. These were of so deep and sacred a character that she could only give them a partial expression, which, however, sufficed to touch her hearers deeply. "They all, with glistening eyes, seemed melted into one love." Hearts were kindled by her utterance to one enthusiasm of sympathy which set out of sight the possibility of future estrangement.

In the conversations of this winter (1840–41) the fine arts held a prominent place.

Margaret stated, at the beginning, that the poetry of life would be found in the advance "from objects to law, from the circumference of being, where we found ourselves at our birth, to the centre." This poetry was "the only path of the true soul," life's prose being the deviation from this ideal way. The fine arts she considered a compensation for this prose, which appeared to her inevitable. The beauties which life could not embody might be expressed in stone, upon canvas, or in music and verse. She did not permit the search for the beautiful to transcend the limits of our social and personal duties. The pursuit of æsthetic pleasure might lead us to fail in attaining the higher beauty. A poetic life was not the life of a *dilettante.*

Of sculpture and music she had much to say, placing them above all other arts. Painting appeared to her inferior to sculpture, because it represented a greater variety of objects, and thus involved more prose. Several conversations were, nevertheless, devoted to Painting, and the conclusion was reached that color was consecrate to passion and sculpture to thought; while yet in some sculptures, like the Niobe, for example, feeling was recognized, but on a grand, universal scale.

The question, "What is life?" occupied one meeting, and brought out many differences of view, which Margaret at last took up into a higher ground, beginning with God as the eternally loving and creating life, and recognizing in human nature a kindred power of love and of creation, through the exercise of which we also add constantly to the total sum of existence, and, leaving behind us ignorance and sin, become godlike in the ability to give, as well as to receive, happiness.

With the work of this winter was combined a series of evening meetings, five in number, to which gentlemen were admitted. Mr. Emerson was present at the second of these, and reports it as having been somewhat encumbered "by the headiness or incapacity of the men," who, as he observes, had not been trained in Margaret's method.

Another chronicler, for whose truth Mr. Emerson vouches, speaks of the plan of these five evenings as a very noble one. They were spoken of as Evenings of Mythology, and Margaret, in devising them, had relied upon the more thorough classical education of the gentlemen to supplement her own knowledge, acquired in a less systematic way. In this hope she was dis-

appointed.   The new-comers did not bring with
them an erudition equal to hers, nor yet any
helpful suggestion of ideas.   The friend whom
we now quote is so much impressed by Margaret's power as to say: "I cannot conceive of
any species of vanity living in her presence.
She distances all who talk with her."   Even Mr.
Emerson served only to display her powers, his
uncompromising idealism seeming narrow and
hard when contrasted with her glowing realism.
"She proceeds in her search after the unity of
things, the divine harmony, not by exclusion, as
Mr. Emerson does, but by comprehension, and
so no poorest, saddest spirit but she will lead to
hope and faith."

Margaret's classes continued through six win-
ters.   The number of those present varied from
twenty-five to thirty.   In 1841–42 the general
subject was Ethics, under which head the Family, the School, the Church, Society, and Literature were all discussed, and with a special reference to "the influences on woman."   In the
winter next after this, we have notes of the following topics: Is the Ideal first or last, Divina-
tion or Experience?   Persons who never awake
to Life in this World; Mistakes; Faith; Creeds;
Woman; Demonology; Influence; Roman Catholicism; The Ideal.

In the season of 1843–44, a number of themes

were considered under the general head of Education. Among these were Culture, Ignorance, Vanity, Prudence, and Patience.

These happy labors came to an end in April of the year 1844, when Margaret parted from her class with many tokens of their love and gratitude. After speaking of affectionate words, beautiful gifts, and rare flowers, she says : —

"How noble has been my experience of such relations now for six years, and with so many and so various minds! Life is worth living, is it not?"

Margaret had answered Mr. Mallock's question before it was asked.

Margaret's summer on the Lakes was the summer of 1843. Her first records of it date from Niagara, and give her impressions of the wonderful scene, in which the rapids impressed her more than the cataract itself, whether seen from the American or from the Canadian side.

"Slowly and thoughtfully I walked down to the bridge leading to Goat Island, and when I stood upon this frail support, and saw a quarter of a mile of tumbling, rushing rapids, and heard their everlasting roar, my emotions overpowered me. A choking sensation rose to my throat, a thrill rushed through my veins, my blood ran rippling to my fingers' ends. This was the climax of the effect which the falls produced upon me."

At Buffalo she embarked for a voyage on Lake Erie. Making a brief stop at Cleveland, the steamer passed on to the St. Clair River. The sight of an encampment of Indians on its bank gave Margaret her first feeling of what was then "the West."

"The people in the boat were almost all New Englanders, seeking their fortunes. They had brought with them their cautious manners, their love of polemics. It grieved me to hear Trinity and Unity discussed in the poor, narrow, doctrinal way on these free waters. But that will soon cease. There is not time for this clash of opinions in the West, where the clash of material interests is so noisy. They will need the spirit of religion more than ever to guide them, but will find less time than before for its doctrine."

The following passage will show us the spirit which Margaret carried into these new scenes : —

"I came to the West prepared for the distaste I must experience at its mushroom growth. I know that where 'Go ahead!' is the motto, the village cannot grow into the gentle proportions that successive lives and the gradations of experience involuntarily give. . . . The march of peaceful, is scarcely less wanton than that of war-

like invention. The old landmarks are broken
down, and the land, for a season, bears none, except of the rudeness of conquest and the needs
of the day. I have come prepared to see all
this, to dislike it, but not with stupid narrowness
to distrust or defame. On the contrary, I trust
by reverent faith to woo the mighty meaning of
the scene, perhaps to foresee the law by which a
new order, a new poetry, is to be evoked from
this chaos."

Charles Dickens's "American Notes" may have
been in Margaret's mind when she penned these
lines, and this faith in her may have been quick-
ened by the perusal of the pages in which he
showed mostly how *not* to see a new country.

Reaching Chicago, she had her first glimpse'
of the prairie, which at first only suggested to
her "the very desolation of dulness."

"After sweeping over the vast monotony of
the Lakes, to come to this monotony of land, with
all around a limitless horizon—to walk and walk,
but never climb! How the eye greeted the approach of a sail or the smoke of a steamboat ; it
seemed that anything so animated must come
from a better land, where mountains give religion to the scene. But after I had ridden out
and seen the flowers, and observed the sun set
with that calmness seen only in the prairies, and
the cattle winding slowly to their homes in the

'island groves,' most peaceful of sights, I began to love, because I began to know, the scene, and shrank no longer from the encircling vastness."

Here followed an excursion of three weeks in a strong wagon drawn by a stalwart pair of horses, and supplied with all that could be needed, as the journey was through Rock River valley, beyond the regions of trade and barter. Margaret speaks of " a guide equally admirable as marshal and companion." This was none other than a younger brother of James Freeman Clarke, William Hull Clarke by name, a man who then and thereafter made Chicago his home, and who lived and died an honored and respected citizen. This journey with Margaret, in which his own sister was of the party, always remained one of the poetic recollections of his early life. He had suffered much from untoward circumstances, and was beginning to lose the elasticity of youth under the burden of his discouragements. Margaret's sympathy divined the depth and delicacy of William Clarke's character, and her unconquerable spirit lifted him from the abyss of despondency into a cheerfulness and courage which nevermore forsook him.

Returning to Chicago, Margaret once more embarked for lake travel, and her next chapter describes Wisconsin, at that time "a Territory,

not yet a State; still nearer the acorn than we
were."

Milwaukee was then a small town, promising,
as she says, "to be, some time, a fine one." The
yellow brick, of which she found it mostly built,
pleased her, as it has pleased the world since.
No railroads with mysterious initials served, in
those days, the needs of that vast region. The
steamer, arriving once in twenty-four hours,
brought mails and travellers, and a little stir
of novelty and excitement. Going a day's journey into the adjacent country, Margaret and her
companions found such accommodation as is
here mentioned : —

"The little log-cabin where we slept, with its
flower-garden in front, disturbed the scene no
more than a lock upon a fair cheek. The hospitality of that house I may well call princely ; it
was the boundless hospitality of the heart, which,
if it has no Aladdin's lamp to create a palace for
the guest, does him still greater service by the
freedom of its bounty to the very last drop of
its powers."

In the Western immigration Milwaukee was
already a station of importance. "Here, on the
pier, I see disembarking the Germans, the Nor-
wegians, the Swedes, the Swiss. Who knows
how much of old legendary lore, of modern wonder, they have already planted amid the Wiscon-

sin forests? Soon their tales of the origin of things, and the Providence that rules them, will be so mingled with those of the Indian that the very oak-tree will not know them apart, will not know whether itself be a Runic, a Druid, or a Winnebago oak."

Margaret reached the island of Mackinaw late in August, and found it occupied by a large representation from the Chippewa and Ottawa tribes, who came there to receive their yearly pension from the Government at Washington. Arriving at night, the steamer fired some rockets, and Margaret heard with a sinking heart the wild cries of the excited Indians, and the pants and snorts of the departing steamer. She walked "with a stranger to a strange hotel," her late companions having gone on with the boat. She found such rest as she could in the room which served at once as sitting and as dining room. The early morning revealed to her the beauties of the spot, and with these the features of her new neighbors.

"With the first rosy streak I was out among my Indian neighbors, whose lodges honeycombed the beautiful beach. They were already on the alert, the children creeping out from beneath the blanket door of the lodge, the women pounding corn in their rude mortars, the young men playing on their pipes. I had been much amused,

when the strain proper to the Winnebago court-
ing flute was played to me on another instrument, at any one's fancying it a melody. But
now, when I heard the notes in their true tone
and time, I thought it not unworthy comparison
with the sweetest bird-song; and this, like the
bird-song, is only practised to allure a mate.
The Indian, become a citizen and a husband, no
more thinks of playing the flute than one of the
settled-down members of our society would of
choosing the purple light of love as dyestuff for
a surtout."

Of the island itself Margaret writes :—

"It was a scene of ideal loveliness, and these
wild forms adorned it, as looking so at home in it."

The Indian encampment was constantly enlarged by new arrivals, which Margaret watched
from the window of her boarding-house.

"I was never tired of seeing the canoes come
in, and the new arrivals set up their temporary
dwellings. The women ran to set up the tent-
poles and spread the mats on the ground. The
men brought the chests, kettles, and so on. The
mats were then laid on the outside, the cedar
boughs strewed on the ground, the blanket hung
up for a door, and all was completed in less than
twenty minutes. Then they began to prepare
the night meal, and to learn of their neighbors
the news of the day."

In these days, in which a spasm of conscience touches the American heart with a sense of the wrongs done to the Indian, Margaret's impressions concerning our aborigines acquire a fresh interest and value. She found them in occupation of many places from which they have since been driven by what is called the march of civilization. We may rather call it a barbarism better armed and informed than their own. She also found among their white neighbors the instinctive dislike and repulsion which are familiar to us. Here, in Mackinaw, Margaret could not consort with them without drawing upon herself the censure of her white acquaintances.

"Indeed, I wonder why they did not give me up, as they certainly looked upon me with great distaste for it. 'Get you gone, you Indian dog!' was the felt, if not the breathed, expression towards the hapless owners of the soil; all their claims, all their sorrows, quite forgot in abhorrence of their dirt, their tawny skins, and the vices the whites have taught them."

Missionary zeal seems to have been at a standstill just at this time, and the hopelessness of converting those heathen to Christianity was held to excuse further effort to that end. Margaret says : —

"Whether the Indian could, by any efforts of love and intelligence, have been civilized and

made a valuable ingredient in the new State, I
will not say ; but this we are sure of, the French
Catholics did not harm them, nor disturb their
minds merely to corrupt them. The French
they loved. But the stern Presbyterian, with
his dogmas and his task-work, the city circle
and the college, with their niggard conceptions
and unfeeling stare, have never tried the experiment."

Margaret naturally felt an especial interest in
observing the character and condition of the
Indian women. She says, truly enough, " The
observations of women upon the position of
woman are always more valuable than those
of men."

Unhappily, this is a theme in regard to which
many women make no observation of their own,
and only repeat what they have heard from men.

But of Margaret's impressions a few sentences
will give us some idea : —

" With the women I held much communication by signs. They are almost invariably coarse
and ugly, with the exception of their eyes, with
a peculiarly awkward gait, and forms bent by
burdens. This gait, so different from the steady
and noble step of the men, marks the inferior
position they occupy."

Margaret quotes from Mrs. Schoolcraft and
from Mrs. Grant passages which assert that this

inferiority does not run through the whole life of an Indian woman, and that the drudgery and weary service imposed upon them by the men are compensated by the esteem and honor in which they are held.   Still, she says : —

" Notwithstanding the homage paid to women, and the consequence allowed them in some cases, it is impossible to look upon the Indian women without feeling that they do occupy a lower place than women among the nations of European civilization. . . . Their decorum and delicacy are striking, and show that, where these are native to the mind, no habits of life make any differ-ence.   Their whole gesture is timid, yet self-possessed.   They used to crowd round me to inspect little things I had to show them, but never press near ; on the contrary, would reprove and keep off the children.   Anything they took from my hand was held with care, then shut or folded, and returned with an air of lady-like pre-cision."

And of the aspect of the Indian question in her day Margaret writes : —

" I have no hope of liberalizing the missionary, of humanizing the sharks of trade, of infusing the conscientious drop into the flinty bosom of policy, of saving the Indian from immediate degrada-tion and speedy death. . . . Yet, let every man look to himself how far this blood shall be re-

quired at his hands. Let the missionary, instead
of preaching to the Indian, preach to the trader
who ruins him, of the dreadful account which
will be demanded of the followers of Cain. Let
every legislator take the subject to heart, and, if
he cannot undo the effects of past sin, try for
that clear view and right sense that may save us
from sinning still more deeply."

Margaret's days in Mackinaw were nine in
number. She went thence by steamer to the
Sault Ste. Marie. On the way thither, the
steamer being detained by a fog, its captain
took her in a small boat to visit the island of
St. Joseph, and on it, the remains of an old
English fort. Her comments upon this visit, in
itself of little interest, are worth quoting : —

"The captain, though he had been on this
trip hundreds of times, had never seen this spot,
and never would but for this fog and his desire to
entertain me. He presented a striking instance
how men, for the sake of getting a living, forget
to live. This is a common fault among the
active men, the truly living, who could tell what
life is. It should not be so. Literature should
not be left to the mere literati, eloquence to the
mere orator. Every Cæsar should be able to
write his own Commentary. We want a more
equal, more thorough, more harmonious development, and there is nothing to hinder the men

of this country from it, except their own supineness or sordid views."

At the Sault, Margaret found many natural beauties, and enjoyed, among other things, the descent of the rapids in a canoe. Returning to Mackinaw, she was joined by her friends, and has further chronicled only her safe return to Buffalo.

The book which preserves the record of this journey saw the light at the end of the next year's summer. Margaret ends it with a little *Envoi* to the reader. But for us, the best *envoi* will be her own description of the last days of its composition : —

" Every day I rose and attended to the many little calls which are always on me, and which have been more of late. Then, about eleven, I would sit down to write at my window, close to which is the apple-tree, lately full of blossoms, and now of yellow-birds.

" Opposite me was Del Sarto's Madonna ; behind me, Silenus, holding in his arms the infant Pan. I felt very content with my pen, my daily bouquet, and my yellow-birds. About five I would go out and walk till dark ; then would arrive my proofs, like crabbed old guardians, coming to tea every night. So passed each day. The 23d of May, my birthday, about one o'clock, I wrote the last line of my little book.

Then I went to Mount Auburn, and walked gently among the graves."

And here ends what we have to say about Margaret's New England life. From its close shelter and intense relations she was now to pass into scenes more varied and labors of a more general scope. She had become cruelly worn by her fatigues in teaching and in writing, and in the year 1844 was induced, by liberal offers, to accept a permanent position on the staff of the "New York Tribune," then in the hands of Messrs. Greeley and McElrath. This step involved the breaking of home ties, and the dispersion of the household which Margaret had done so much to sustain and to keep together. Margaret's brothers had now left college, and had betaken themselves to the pursuits chosen as their life work. Her younger sister was married, and it was decided that her mother should divide her time among these members of her family, leaving Margaret free to begin a new season of work under circumstances which promised her greater freedom from care and from the necessity of unremitting exertion.

CHAPTER VIII.

FAREWELL TO BOSTON. — ENGAGEMENT TO WRITE FOR
THE "NEW YORK TRIBUNE." — MARGARET IN HER
NEW SURROUNDINGS. — MR. GREELEY'S OPINION OF
MARGARET'S WORK. — HER ESTIMATE OF GEORGE
SAND.

WHEN Margaret stepped for the last time across
the threshold of her mother's home, she must
have had the rare comfort of knowing that she
had done everything in her power to promote
the highest welfare of those who, with her, had
shared its shelter. The children of the household had grown up under her fostering care, nor
had she, in any flight of her vivid imagination,
forgotten the claims and needs of brothers. sister, or mother. So closely, indeed, had she felt
herself bound by the necessity of doing what was
best for each and all, that her literary work had
not, in any degree, corresponded to her own desires. Her written and spoken word had indeed
carried with it a quickening power for good; but
she had not been able so much as to plan one of
the greater works which she considered herself
bound to produce, and which could neither have

been conceived nor carried out without ample command of time and necessary conditions. In a letter written to one of her brothers at this time, Margaret says : —

"If our family affairs could now be so arranged that I might be tolerably tranquil for the next six or eight years, I should go out of life better satisfied with the page I have turned in it than I shall if I must still toil on. A noble career is yet before me, if I can be unimpeded by cares. I have given almost all my young energies to personal relations ; but at present I feel inclined to impel the general stream of thought. Let my nearest friends also wish that I should now take share in more public life."

The opening now found for Margaret in New York, though fortunate, was by no means fortuitous. She had herself prepared the way thereunto by her good work in the " Dial." In that cheerless editorial seat she may sometimes, like the Lady of Shalott, have sighed to see Sir Lancelot ride careless by, or with the spirit of an unrecognized prophet she may have exclaimed, "Who hath believed our report ? " But her word had found one who could hear it to some purpose.

Mr. Greeley had been, from the first, a reader of this periodical, and had recognized the fresh

9

thought and new culture which gave it character. His attention was first drawn to Margaret by an essay of hers, published in the July number of 1843, and entitled "The Great Lawsuit, — Man *versus* Men, Woman *versus* Women." This essay, which at a later date expanded into the volume known as "Woman in the Nineteenth Century," struck Mr. Greeley as "the production of an original, vigorous, and earnest mind." Margaret's "Summer on the Lakes" appeared also in the "Dial" somewhat later, and was considered by Mr. Greeley as "unequalled, especially in its pictures of the prairies and of the sunnier aspects of pioneer life." Convinced of the literary ability of the writer, he gave ear to a suggestion of Mrs. Greeley, and, in accordance with her wishes and with his own judgment, extended to her the invitation already spoken of as accepted.

This invitation, and the arrangement to which it led, admitted Margaret not only to the columns of the "Tribune," but also to the home of its editor, in which she continued to reside during the period of her connection with the paper. This home was in a spacious, old-fashioned house on the banks of the East River, completely secluded by the adjacent trees and garden, but within easy reach of New York by car and omnibus. Margaret came there in December, 1844, and was at once struck with the beauty of the scene and charmed with the aspect of the antiquated dwelling, which had once, no doubt, been the villa of some magnate of old New York.

If the outside world of the time troubled itself at all about the Greeley household, it must have considered it in the light of a happy family of eccentrics. Upon the personal peculiarities of Mr. Greeley we need not here enlarge. They were of little account in comparison with the character of the man, who himself deserved the name which he gave to his paper, and was at heart a tribune of the people. Mrs. Greeley was herself a woman of curious theories, and it is probable that Margaret, in her new surroundings, found herself obliged in a certain degree to represent the conventional side of life, which her host and hostess were inclined to disregard.

By Mr. Greeley's own account there were differences between Margaret and himself regarding a great variety of subjects, including the use of tea and coffee, which he eschewed and to which she adhered, and the emancipation of women, to which Mr. Greeley proposed to attach, as a condition, the abrogation of such small courtesies as are shown the sex to-day, while Margaret demanded a greater deference as a concomitant of the larger liberty. Mr. Greeley at first determined to keep beyond the sphere of

Margaret's fascination, and to burn no incense at her shrine. She appeared to him somewhat spoiled by the "Oriental adoration" which she received from other women, themselves persons of character and of culture. Her foibles impressed him as much as did the admirable qualities which he was forced to recognize in her. Vain resolution! Living under the same roof with Margaret, he could not but come to know her, and, knowing her, he had no choice but to join the throng of her admirers. To him, as to others, the blemishes at first discerned " took on new and brighter aspects in the light of her radiant and lofty soul."

" I learned," says Mr. Greeley, "to know her as a most fearless and unselfish champion of truth and human good at all hazards, ready to be their standard-bearer through danger and obloquy, and, if need be, their martyr."

Mr. Greeley bears witness also to the fact that this ready spirit of self-sacrifice in Margaret did not spring either from any asceticism of temperament or from an undervaluation of material advantages. Margaret, he thinks, appreciated fully all that riches, rank, and luxury could give. She prized all of these in their place, but prized far above them all the opportunity to serve and help her fellow-creatures.

The imperative drill of press-work was new

and somewhat irksome to her. She was accustomed indeed to labor in season and out of season, and in so doing to struggle with bodily pain and weariness. But to take up the pen at the word of command, without the interior bidding of the divine afflatus, was a new necessity, and one to which she found it difficult to submit. Mr. Greeley prized her work highly, though with some drawbacks. He could not always command it at will, for the reason that she could not. He found her writing, however, terse, vigorous, and practical, and considered her contributions to the " Tribune " more solid in merit, though less ambitious in scope, than her essays written earlier for the " Dial." Margaret herself esteemed them but moderately, feeling that she had taken up this new work at a time when her tired faculties needed rest and recreation.

In a brief memorial of Margaret, Mr. Greeley gives us the titles of the most important of these papers. They are as follows: " Thomas Hood," " Edgar A. Poe," " Capital Punishment," " Cassius M. Clay," " New Year's Day," " Christmas," " Thanksgiving," " St. Valentine's," " Fourth of July," " The First of August " — which she commemorates as the anniversary of slave-emancipation in the British West Indies.

In looking over the volumes which contain these and many others of Margaret's collected

papers, we are carried back to a time in which
issues now long settled were in the early stages
of their agitation, and in which many of those
whom we now most revere in memory were living actors on the stage of the century's life.
Hawthorne and Longfellow were then young
writers. The second series of Mr. Emerson's
"Essays" is noticed as of recent publication. At
the time of her writing, it would seem that Mr.
Emerson had a larger circle of readers in England
than in his own country. She accounts for this
on the ground that "our people, heated by a partisan spirit, necessarily occupied in these first stages
by bringing out the material resources of the
land, not generally prepared by early training for
the enjoyment of books that require attention
and reflection, are still more injured by a large
majority of writers and speakers who lend all
their efforts to flatter corrupt tastes and mental
indolence." She permits us, however, to "hail
as an auspicious omen the influence Mr. Emerson has obtained" in New England, which she
recognizes as deep-rooted, and, over the younger
part of the community, far greater than that of
any other person. She is glad to introduce Robert
Browning as the author of "Bells and Pome-
granates" to the American public. Mrs. Browning was then Miss Barrett, in regard of whom
Margaret rejoices that her task is "mainly to

express a cordial admiration !" and says that she "cannot hesitate to rank her, in vigor and nobleness of conception, depth of spiritual experience, and command of classic allusion, above any female writer the world has yet known." In those poems of hers which emulate Milton and Dante " her success is far below what we find in the poems of feeling and experience; for she has the vision of a great poet, but little in proportion of his classic power."

Margaret has much to say concerning George Sand, and under various heads. In her work on Woman, she gives the *rationale* of her strange and anomalous appearance, and is at once very just and very tender in her judgments.

George Sand was then in the full bloom of her reputation. The light and the shade of her character, as known to the public, were at the height of their contrast. To the literary merit of her work was added the interest of a mysterious personality, which rebelled against the limits of sex, and, not content to be either man or woman, touched with a new and strange protest the imagination of the time.

The inexorable progress of events has changed this, with so much else. Youth, beauty, sex, all imperial in their day, are discrowned by the dusty hand of Time, and ranged in the gallery of the things that were. George Sand's volumes

still glow and sparkle on the bookshelf ; but
George Sand's personality and her passions are
dim visions of the past, and touch us no longer.
When Margaret wrote of her, the woman was
at the zenith of her power, and the intoxication
of her influence was so great that a calm judgment
concerning it was difficult.   Like a wild Bacchante, she led her chorus of bold spirits through
the formal ways of French society, which in her
view were bristling with pruriency and veiled with
hypocrisy.   Like Margaret's, her cry was, "Truth
at all hazards!"   But hers was not the ideal
truth which Margaret followed so zealously.
"So vile are men, so weak are women, so ruthless is passion," were the utterances of her sincerity.   Mistress of the revels, she did indeed
command a new unmasking at the banquet,
thoughtless of the risk of profaning innocent
imaginations with sad facts which they had no
need to know, and which, shown by such a master
of art and expression, might bear with them the
danger fabled in the mingled beauty and horror
of the Gorgon's head.

George Sand was saved by the sincerity of her
intention.   Her somnambulic utterances had told
of her good faith, and of her belief in things truly
human and divine. Her revolutionary indignation
was against the really false and base, and her progress was to a position from which she was able

calmly to analyze and loftily to repudiate the dis-
orders in which she was supposed to have lost
for a time the sustaining power of reason and
self-command.

To those of us who remember these things in
the vividness of their living presence, it is most
satisfactory to be assured of the excellence of
Margaret's judgment. The great Frenchwo-
man, at the period of which we write, appeared
to many the incarnation of all the evil which her
sex could represent. To those of opposite mind
she appeared the inspired prophetess of a new
era of thought and of sentiment. To Margaret
she was neither the one nor the other. Much as
she loved genius, that of George Sand could not
blind her to the faults and falsities that marred
her work. Stern idealist as she was, the most
objectionable part of Madame Sand's record
could not move her to a moment's injustice or
uncharity in her regard.

In "Woman in the Nineteenth Century" Margaret says : —

" George Sand smokes, wears male attire,
wishes to be addressed as *mon frère*. Perhaps,
if she found those who were as brothers indeed,
she would not care whether she were brother or
sister."

And concerning her writings : —

" This author, beginning like the many in as-sault upon bad institutions and external ills, yet deepening the experience through comparative freedom, sees at last that the only efficient remedy must come from individual character.

"The mind of the age struggles confusedly with these problems, better discerning as yet the ill it can no longer bear than the good by which it may supersede it. But women like Sand will speak now, and cannot be silenced ; their characters and their eloquence alike foretell an era when such as they shall easier learn to lead true lives. But though such forebode, not such shall be parents of it. Those who would reform the world must show that they do not speak in the heat of wild impulse ; their lives must be unstained by passionate error. They must be religious students of the Divine purpose with regard to man, if they would not confound the fancies of a day with the requisitions of eternal good."

So much for the woman Sand, as known to Margaret through her works and by hearsay. Of the writer she first knew through her "Seven Strings of the Lyre," a rhapsodic sketch. Margaret prizes in this "the knowledge of the passions and of social institutions, with the celestial choice which was above them." In the romances "André" and "Jacques" she traces "the same high morality of one who had tried the liberty of circumstance only to learn to appreciate the liberty of law. . . . Though the sophistry of passion in these books disgusted me, flowers of purest hue seemed to grow upon the dark and dirty ground. I thought she had cast aside the slough of her past life, and begun a new existence beneath the sun of a new ideal." The "Lettres d'un Voyageur" seem to Margaret shallow, — the work of "a frail woman mourning over her lot." But when "Consuelo" appears, she feels herself strengthened in her first interpretation of George Sand's true character, and takes her stand upon the "original nobleness and love of right" which even the wild impulses of her fiery blood were never able entirely to oversweep. Of the work itself she says : —

"To many women this picture will prove a true *consuelo* (consolation), and we think even very prejudiced men will not read it without being charmed with the expansion, sweetness, and genuine force of a female character such as they have not met, but must, when painted, recognize as possible, and may be led to review their opinions, and perhaps to elevate and enlarge their hopes, as to 'woman's sphere' and 'woman's mission.'"

CHAPTER IX.

WE have no very full record of Margaret's life
beneath the roof of the Greeley mansion. The
information that we can gather concerning it
seems to indicate that it was, on the whole, a
period of rest and of enlargement. True, her
task-work continued without intermission, and
her incitements to exertion were not fewer than
in the past. But the change of scene and of
occupation gives refreshment, if not repose, to
minds of such activity, and Margaret, accustomed to the burden of constant care and anxiety, was now relieved from much of this. She
relied much, and with reason, both upon Mr.
Greeley's judgment and upon his friendship.
The following extract from a letter to her

brother Eugene gives us an inkling as to her first impressions : —

" The place where we live is old and dilapidated, but in a situation of great natural loveliness. When there I am perfectly secluded, yet every one I wish to see comes to see me, and I can get to the centre of the city in half an hour. Here is all affection for me and desire to make me at home ; and I do feel so, which could scarcely have been expected from such an arrangement. My room is delightful ; how I wish you could sit at its window with me, and see the sails glide by !

" As to the public part, that is entirely satisfactory. I do just as I please, and as much and as little as I please, and the editors express themselves perfectly satisfied, and others say that my pieces *tell* to a degree I could not expect. I think, too, I shall do better and better. I am truly interested in this great field which opens before me, and it is pleasant to be sure of a chance at half a hundred thousand readers."

The enlargement spoken of above was found by Margaret in her more varied field of literary action, and in the society of a city which had, even at that date, a cosmopolitan, semi-European character.

New York has always, with a little grumbling,

conceded to Boston the palm of literary prece-
dence. In spite of this, there has always been
a good degree of friendly intercourse among its
busy *littérateurs* and artists, who find, in the
more vivid movement and wider market of the
larger city, a compensation, if not an equivalent,
for its distance from the recognized centres of
intellectual influence.

In these circles Margaret was not only a welcome, but a desired guest. In the *salons* of the
time she had the position of a celebrity. Here,
as elsewhere, her twofold magnetism strongly
attracted some and repelled others. Somewhat
hypercritical and pedantic she was judged to be
by those who observed her at a distance, or
heard from her only a chance remark. Such an
observer, admiring but not approaching, saw at
times the look of the sibyl flash from beneath
Margaret's heavy eyelids ; and once, hearing
her sigh deeply after a social evening, was moved
to ask her why. "Alone, as usual!" was Margaret's answer, with one or two pathetic words,
the remembrance of which brought tears to
the eyes of the person to whom they were
spoken.

In these days she wrote in her journal : —

"There comes a consciousness that I have no
real hold on life, — no real, permanent connection with any soul. I seem a wandering Intel-

ligence, driven from spot to spot, that I may
learn all secrets, and fulfil a circle of knowledge. This thought envelops me as a cold
atmosphere."

From this chill isolation of feeling Margaret
was sometimes relieved by the warm appreciation of those whom she had truly found, of
whom one could say to her: "You come like
one of the great powers of nature, harmonizing
with all beauty of the soul or of the earth. You
cannot be discordant with anything that is true
or deep."

Other neighbors, and of a very different character, had Margaret in her new surroundings.
The prisons at Blackwell's Island were on the
opposite side of the river, at a distance easily
reached by boat. Sing Sing prison was not far
off; and Margaret accepted the invitation to
pass a Sunday within its walls. She had con-
sorted hitherto with the *élite* of her sex, the
women attracted to her having invariably been
of a superior type. She now made acquaintance
with the outcasts in whom the elements of
womanhood are scarcely recognized. For both
she had one gospel, that of high hope and
divine love. She seems to have found herself
as much at home in the office of encouraging
the fallen, as she had been when it was her duty
to arouse the best spirit in women sheltered

from the knowledge and experience of evil by every favoring circumstance.

This was in the days in which Judge Edmonds had taken great interest in the affairs of the prison. Mrs. Farnum, a woman of uncommon character and ability, had charge of the female prisoners, who already showed the results of her intelligent and kindly treatment. On the occasion of her first visit, Margaret spoke with only a few of the women, and says that "the interview was very pleasant. These women were all from the lowest haunts of vice, yet nothing could have been more decorous than their conduct, while it was also frank. *All passed, indeed, much as in one of my Boston classes.*"

This last phrase may somewhat startle us ; but it should only assure us that Margaret had found, in confronting two circles so widely dissimilar, the happy words which could bring high and low into harmony with the true divine.

Margaret's second visit to the prison was on the Christmas soon following. She was invited to address the women in their chapel, and has herself preserved some record of her discourse, which was extemporaneous. Seated at the desk, no longer with the critical air which repelled the timid, but deeply penetrated by the pathos of the occasion, she began with the words, "To me the pleasant office has been given of wishing you a happy Christmas." And the sad assembly smiled, murmuring its thanks. What a Christ-like power was that which brought this sun-gleam of a smile into that dark tragedy of offence and punishment !

Some passages of this address must be given here, to show the attitude in which this truly noble woman confronted the most degraded of her sex. After alluding to the common opinion that "women once lost are far worse than abandoned men, and cannot be restored," she said : —

"It is not so. I know my sex better. It is because women have so much feeling, and such a rooted respect for purity, that they seem so shameless and insolent when they feel that they have erred, and that others think ill of them. When they meet man's look of scorn, the desperate passion that rises is a perverted pride, which might have been their guardian angel. Rather let me say, which may be ; for the rapid improvement wrought here gives us warm hopes."

Margaret exhorts the prisoners not to be impatient for their release. She dwells upon their weakness, the temptations of the outer world, and the helpful character of the influences which are now brought to bear upon them.

"Oh, be sure that you are fitted to triumph

over evil before you again expose yourselves to
it! Instead of wasting your time and strength
in vain wishes, use this opportunity to prepare
yourselves for a better course of life when you
are set free."

The following sentences are also noteworthy:

" Let me warn you earnestly against acting
insincerely. I know you must prize the good
opinion of your friendly protectors, but do not
buy it at the cost of truth. Try to be, not to
seem. . . . Never despond, — never say, ' It is too
late!' Fear not, even if you relapse again and
again. If you fall, do not lie grovelling, but rise
upon your feet once more, and struggle bravely
on. And if aroused conscience makes you suffer
keenly, have patience to bear it. God will not
let you suffer more than you need to fit you for
his grace. . . . Cultivate this spirit of prayer. I
do not mean agitation and excitement, but a deep
desire for truth, purity, and goodness."

Margaret visited also the prisons on Blackwell's Island, and, walking through the women's
hospital, shed the balm of her presence upon the
most hardened of its wretched inmates. She
had always wished to have a better understanding of the feelings and needs of "those women
who are trampled in the mud to gratify the brute
appetites of men," in order to lend them a helping hand.

The following extracts from letters, hitherto in great part unpublished, will give the reader some idea of Margaret's tender love and care for the dear ones from whom she was now separated. The letters are mostly addressed to her younger brother, Richard, and are dated in various epochs of the year 1845. One of these recalls her last impressions in leaving Boston : —

" The last face I saw in Boston was Anna Loring's, looking after me from Dr. Peabody's steps. Mrs. Peabody stood behind her, some way up, nodding adieux to the 'darling,' as she addressed me, somewhat to my emotion. They seemed like a frosty November afternoon and a soft summer twilight, when night's glorious star begins to shine.

" When you go to Mrs. Loring's, will you ask W. Story if he has any of Robert Browning's poems to lend me for a short time ? They shall be returned safe. I only want them a few days, to make some extracts for the paper. They cannot be obtained here."

The following extracts refer to the first appearance of her book, "Woman in the Nineteenth Century." Her brother Eugene had found a notice of it in some remote spot. She writes : —

" It was pleasant you should see that little notice in that wild place. The book is out, and the theme of all the newspapers and many of the journals. Abuse, public and private, is lavished upon its views, but respect is expressed for me personally. But the most speaking fact, and the one which satisfied me, is, that the whole edition was sold off in a week to the booksellers, and eighty-five dollars handed to me as my share. Not that my object was in any wise money, but I consider this the signet of success. If one can be heard, that is enough."

In August, 1845, she writes thus to Richard:

" I really loathe my pen at present; it is entirely unnatural to me to keep at it so in the summer. Looking at these dull blacks and whites so much, when nature is in her bright colors, is a source of great physical weariness and irritation. I cannot, therefore, write you good letters, but am always glad to get them.

" As to what you say of my writing books, that cannot be at present. I have not health and energy to do so many things, and find too much that I value in my present position to give it up rashly or suddenly. But doubt not, as I do not, that Heaven has good things enough for me to do, and that I shall find them best by not exhausting or overstraining myself."

To Richard she writes, some months later: —

" I have to-day the unexpected pleasure of

receiving from England a neat copy of ' Woman in the Nineteenth Century,' republished there in Clark's 'Cabinet Library.' I had never heard a word about it from England, and am very glad to find it will be read by women there. As to advantage to me, the republication will bring me no money, but will be of use to me here, as our dear country folks look anxiously for verdicts from the other side of the water.

" I shall get out a second edition before long, I hope; and wish you would translate for me, and send those other parts of the story of ' Panthea' you thought I might like."

The extract subjoined will show Margaret's anxious thought concerning her mother's comfort and welfare. It is addressed to the same brother, whom she thus admonishes : —

" She speaks of you most affectionately, but happened to mention that you took now no interest in a garden. I have known you would do what you thought of to be a good son, and not neglect your positive duties; but I have feared you would not show enough of sympathy with her tastes and pursuits. Care of the garden *is* a way in which you could give her genuine comfort and pleasure, while regular exercise in it would be of great use to yourself. Do not neglect this nor any the most trifling attention she may wish ; because it is not by attending to

our friends in our way, but in *theirs*, that we
can really avail them. I think of you much with
love and pride and hope for your public and
private life."

Margaret's preface to "Woman in the Nineteenth Century" bears the date of November,
1844. The greater part of the work, as has
already been said, had appeared in the "Dial,"
under a different title, for which she in this
place expresses a preference, as better suited to
the theme she proposes to treat of. "Man versus
Men, Woman versus Women," means to her the
leading idea and ideal of humanity,, as wrónged
and hindered from development by the thoughtless and ignorant action of the race itself. The
title finally given was adopted in accordance
with the wishes of friends, who thought the
other wanting in clearness. "By man, I mean
both man and woman : these are the two halves
of one thought. I lay no especial stress on the
welfare of either. I believe that the development of the one cannot be effected without that
of the other."

In the name of a common humanity, then,
Margaret solicits from her readers "a sincere
and patient attention," praying women particularly to study for themselves the freedom which
the law should secure to them. It is this that

she seeks, not to be replaced by "the largest extension of partial privileges."

"And may truth, unpolluted by prejudice, vanity, or selfishness, be granted daily more and more, as the due inheritance and only valuable conquest for us all!"

The leading thought formulated by Margaret in the title of her preference is scarcely carried out in her work; at least, not with any systematic parallelism. Her study of the position and possibilities of woman is not the less one of unique value and interest. The work shows throughout the grasp and mastery of her mind. Her faith in principles, her reliance upon them in the interpretation of events, make her strong and bold. We do not find in this book one careless expression which would slur over the smallest detail of womanly duty, or absolve from the attainment of any or all of the feminine graces. Of these, Margaret deeply knows the value. But, in her view, these duties will never be noble, these graces sincere, until women stand as firmly as men do upon the ground of individual freedom and legal justice.

"If principles could be established, particulars would adjust themselves aright. Ascertain the true destiny of woman; give her legitimate hopes, and a standard within herself. . . . What woman needs is not as a woman to act or rule, but as a nature to grow, as an intellect to discern, as a soul to live freely and unimpeded."

She would have " every arbitrary barrier thrown down, every path laid open to woman as freely as to man." And she insists that this " inward and outward freedom shall be acknowledged as a *right*, not yielded as a concession."

The limits of our present undertaking do not allow us to give here an extended notice of this work, which has long belonged to general literature, and is, perhaps, the most widely known of Margaret's writings. We must, however, dwell sufficiently upon its merits to commend it to the men and women of to-day, as equally interesting to both, and as entirely appropriate to the standpoint of the present time.

Nothing that has been written or said, in later days, has made its teaching superfluous. It demands all that is asked to-day for women, and that on the broadest and most substantial ground. The usual arguments against the emancipation of women from a position of political and social inferiority are all carefully considered and carefully answered. Much study is shown of the prominent women of history, and of the condition of the sex at different periods. Much understanding also of the ideal womanhood, which has always had its place in the van of human progress, and of the actual womanhood, which has mostly been bred and trained in an opposite direction.

We have, then, in the book, a thorough state-ment, both of the shortcomings of women them-selves, and of the wrongs which they in turn suffer from society. The cause of the weak against the strong is advanced with sound and rational argument. We will not say that a thoughtful reader of to-day will indorse every word of this remarkable treatise. Its fervor here and there runs into vague enthusiasm, and much is asserted about souls and their future which thinkers of the present day do not so confidently assume to know.

The extent of Margaret's reading is shown in her command of historical and mythical illus-tration. Her beloved Greeks furnish her with some portraits of ideal men in relation with ideal women. As becomes a champion, she knows the friends and the enemies of the cause which she makes her own. Here, for example, is a fine discrimination : —

" The spiritual tendency is toward the eleva-tion of woman, but the intellectual, by itself, is not so. Plato sometimes seems penetrated by that high idea of love which considers man and woman as the twofold expression of one thought. But then again Plato, the man of intellect, treats woman in the republic as property, and in the

" Timæus " says that man, if he misuse the privileges of one life, shall be degraded into the form of a woman."

Margaret mentions among the women whom she considered helpers and favorers of the new womanhood, Miss Edgeworth, Mrs. Jameson, and our own Miss Sedgwick. Among the writers of the other sex, whose theories point to the same end, she speaks of Swedenborg, Fourier, and Goethe. The first-named comes to this through his mystical appreciation of spiritual life ; the second, by his systematic distribution of gifts and opportunities according to the principles of ideal justice. The world-wise Goethe everywhere recognizes the presence and significance of the feminine principle ; and, after treating with tenderness and reverence its frailest as well as its finest impersonations, lays the seal of all attraction in the lap of the " eternal womanly."

Nearer at hand, and in the intimacy of personal intercourse, Margaret found a noble friend to her cause.

" The late Dr. Channing, whose enlarged and religious nature shared every onward impulse of his time, though his thoughts followed his wishes with a deliberative caution which belonged to his habits and temperament, was greatly interested in these expectations for women. He regarded them as souls, each of which had a destiny of its own, incalculable to other minds, and whose leading it must follow, guided by the light of a private conscience."

She tells us that the Doctor's delicate and fastidious taste was not shocked by Angelina Grimké's appearance in public, and that he fully indorsed Mrs. Jameson's defence of her sex " in a way from which women usually shrink, because, if they express themselves on such subjects with sufficient force and clearness to do any good, they are exposed to assaults whose vulgarity makes them painful."

Margaret ends her treatise with a synopsis of her humanitarian creed, of which we can here give only enough to show its general scope and tenor. Here is the substance of it, mostly in her own words : —

Man is a being of twofold relations, — to nature beneath and intelligences above him. The earth is his school, God his object, life and thought his means of attaining it.

The growth of man is twofold, — masculine and feminine. These terms, for Margaret, represent other qualities, to wit, Energy and Harmony, Power and Beauty, Intellect and Love.

These faculties belong to both sexes, yet the two are distinguished by the preponderance of the opposing characteristics.

Were these opposites in perfect harmony, they would respond to and complete each other.

Why does this harmony not prevail?

Because, as man came before woman, power before beauty, he kept his ascendency, and enslaved her.

Woman in turn rose by her moral power, which a growing civilization recognized.

Man became more just and kind, but failed to see that woman was half himself, and that, by the laws of their common being, he could never reach his true proportions while she remained shorn of hers. And so it has gone on to our day.

Pure love, poetic genius, and true religion have done much to vindicate and to restore the normal harmony.

The time has now come when a clearer vision and better action are possible, — when man and woman may stand as pillars of one temple, priests of one worship.

This hope should attain its amplest fruition in our own country, and will do so if the principles from which sprang our national life are adhered to.

Women should now be the best helpers of women. Of men, we need only ask the removal of arbitrary barriers.

The question naturally suggests itself, What use will woman make of her liberty after so many ages of restraint?

Margaret says, in answer, that this freedom
will not be immediately given. But, even if it
were to come suddenly, she finds in her own
sex " a reverence for decorums and limits inher-
ited and enhanced from generation to generation, which years of other life could not efface."
She believes, also, that woman as woman is
characterized by a native love of proportion, —
a Greek moderation, — which would immediately create a restraining party, and would gradually establish such rules as are needed to guard
life without impeding it.

This opinion of Margaret's is in direct contra-
diction to one very generally held to-day, namely,
that women tend more to extremes than men
do, and are often seen to exaggerate to irrational
frenzy the feelings which agitate the male portion of the community. The reason for this, if
honestly sought, can easily be found. Women
in whom the power of individual judgment has
been either left without training or forcibly suppressed will naturally be led by impulse and
enthusiasm, and will be almost certain to in-
flame still further the kindled passions of the
men to whom they stand related. Margaret
knew this well enough ; but she had also known
women of a very different type, who had trained
and disciplined themselves by the help of that
nice sense of measure which belongs to any

normal human intelligence, and which, in women, is easily reached and rendered active. It
was upon this best and wisest womanhood that
Margaret relied for the standard which should
redeem the sex from violence and headlong excitement. Here, as elsewhere, she shows her
faith in the good elements of human nature, and
sees them, in her prophetic vision, as already
crowned with an enduring victory.

"I stand in the sunny noon of life. Objects
no longer glitter in the dews of morning, neither are yet softened by the shadows of evening. Every spot is seen, every chasm revealed.
Climbing the dusty hill, some fair effigies that
once stood for human destiny have been broken.
Yet enough is left to point distinctly to the glories of that destiny."

Margaret gives us, as the end of the whole
matter, this sentence : —

"Always the soul says to us all, Cherish your
best hopes as a faith, and abide by them in action. . . . Such shall be the effectual fervent
means to their fulfilment."

In this sunny noon of life things new and
strange were awaiting Margaret. Her days
among kindred and country-people were nearly
ended. The last volume given by her to the
American public was entitled " Papers on Art
and Literature." Of these, a number had al-

ready appeared in print. In her preface she mentions the essay on " American Literature " as one now published for the first time, and also as " a very imperfect sketch," which she hopes to complete by some later utterance. She commends it to us, however, as " written with sincere and earnest feelings, and from a mind that cares for nothing but what is permanent and essential." She thinks it should, therefore, have " some merit, if only in the power of suggestion." It has for us the great interest of making known Margaret's opinion of her compeers in literature, and with her appreciation of these, not always just or adequate, her views of the noble national life to which American literature, in its maturer growth, should give expression.

Margaret says, at the outset, that " some thinkers " may accuse her of writing about a thing that does not exist. " For," says she, " it does not follow, because many books are written by persons born in America, that there exists an American literature. Books which imitate or represent the thoughts and life of Europe do not constitute an American literature. Before such can exist, an original idea must animate this nation, and fresh currents of life must call into life fresh thoughts along its shores."

In reviewing these first sentences, we are led to say that they partly commend themselves to our judgment, and partly do not. Here, as in much that Margaret has written, a solid truth is found side by side with an illusion. The statement that an American idea should lie at the foundation of our national life and its expression is a truth too often lost sight of by those to whom it most imports. On the other hand, the great body of the world's literature is like an ocean in whose waves and tides there is a continuity which sets at naught the imposition of definite limits. Literature is first of all human ; and American books, which express human thought, feeling, and experience, are American literature, even if they show no distinctive national feature.

In what follows, Margaret confesses that her own studies have been largely of the classics of foreign countries. She has found, she says, a model "in the simple masculine minds of the great Latin authors." She has observed, too, the features of kindred between the character of the ancient Roman and that of the Briton of to-day.

She remarks upon the reaction which was felt in her time against the revolutionary opposition to the mother country. This reaction, she feels, may be carried too far.

"What suits Great Britain, with her insular position and consequent need to concentrate and intensify her life, her limited monarchy and spirit of trade, does not suit a mixed race, continually enriched (?) with new blood from other stocks the most unlike that of our first descent, with ample field and verge enough to range in and leave every impulse free, and abundant opportunity to develop a genius wide and full as our rivers, luxuriant and impassioned as our vast prairies, rooted in strength as the rocks on which the Puritan fathers landed."

Margaret anticipates for this Western hemisphere the rise and development of such a genius, but says that this cannot come until the fusion of races shall be more advanced, nor "until this nation shall attain sufficient moral and intellectual dignity to prize moral and intellectual no less highly than political freedom."

She finds the earnest of this greater time in the movements already leading to social reforms, and in the " stern sincerity " of elect individuals, but thinks that the influences at work " must go deeper before **we** can have poets."

At the time of her writing (1844–45) she considers literature as in a "dim and struggling state," with " pecuniary results exceedingly pitiful. The state of things gets worse and worse, as less and less is offered for works demanding great devotion of time and labor, and the publisher, obliged to regard the transaction as a matter of business, demands of the author only what will find an immediate market, for he cannot afford to take anything else."

Margaret thinks that matters were better in this respect during the first half-century of our republican existence. The country was not then "so deluged with the dingy page reprinted from Europe." Nor did Americans fail to answer sharply the question, "Who reads an American book?" But the books of that period, to which she accords much merit, seem to her so reflected from England in their thought and inspiration, that she inclines to call them English rather than American.

Having expressed these general views, Margaret proceeds to pass in review the prominent American writers of the time, beginning with the department of history. In this she accords to Prescott industry, the choice of valuable material, and the power of clear and elegant arrangement. She finds his books, however, "wonderfully tame," and characterized by "the absence of thought." In Mr. Bancroft she recognizes a writer of a higher order, possessed of "leading thoughts, by whose aid he groups his facts." Yet, by her own account, she has read him less diligently than his brother historian.

In ethics and philosophy she mentions, as

"likely to live and be blessed and honored in the later time," the names of Channing and Emerson. Of the first she says: "His leading idea of the dignity of human nature is one of vast results, and the peculiar form in which he advocated it had a great work to do in this new world. . . . On great questions he took middle ground, and sought a panoramic view. . . . He was not well acquainted with man on the impulsive and passionate side of his nature, so that his view of character was sometimes narrow, but always noble."

Margaret turns from the great divine to her Concord friend as one turns from shade to sunshine. "The two men are alike," she says, "in dignity of purpose, disinterest, and purity." But of the two she recognizes Mr. Emerson as the profound thinker and man of ideas, dealing "with causes rather than with effects." His influence appears to her deep, not wide, but constantly extending its circles. He is to her "a harbinger of the better day."

Irving, Cooper, Miss Sedgwick, and Mrs. Child are briefly mentioned, but with characteristic appreciation. "The style of story current in the magazines" is pronounced by her "flimsy beyond any texture that was ever spun or dreamed of by the mind of man."

Our friend now devotes herself to the poets of

America, at whose head she places " Mr. Bryant, alone." Genuineness appears to be his chief merit, in her eyes, for she does not find his genius either fertile or comprehensive. " But his poetry is purely the language of his inmost nature, and the simple, lovely garb in which his thoughts are arrayed, a direct gift from the Muse."

Halleck, Willis, and Dana receive each their meed of praise at her hands. Passing over what is said, and well said, of them, we come to a criticism on Mr. Longfellow, which is much at variance with his popular reputation, and which, though acute and well hit, will hardly commend itself to-day to the judgment either of the learned or unlearned. For, even if Mr. Longfellow's inspiration be allowed to be a reflected rather than an original one, the mirror of his imagination is so pure and broad, and the images it reflects are so beautiful, that the world of our time confesses itself greatly his debtor. The spirit of his life, too, has put the seal of a rare earnestness and sincerity upon his legacy to the world of letters. But let us hear Margaret's estimate of him : —

" Longfellow is artificial and imitative. He borrows incessantly, and mixes what he borrows, so that it does not appear to the best advantage. . . . The ethical part of his writing has a hollow, second-hand sound. He has, however, elegance, a love of the beautiful, and a fancy for what is large and manly, if not a full sympathy with it. His verse breathes at times much sweetness. Though imitative, he is not mechanical."

In an article of some length, printed in connection with this, but first published in the "New York Tribune," Margaret's dispraise of this poet is in even larger proportion to her scant commendation of him. This review was called forth by the appearance of an illustrated edition of Mr. Longfellow's poems, most of which had already appeared in smaller volumes, and in the Annuals, which once figured so largely in the show-æsthetics of society. Mr. Greeley, in some published reminiscences, tells us that Margaret undertook this task with great reluctance. He, on the other hand, was too much overwhelmed with business to give the volume proper notice, and so persuaded Margaret to deal with it as she could.

After formulating a definition of poetry which she considers "large enough to include all excellence," she laments the dearth of true poetry, and asserts that "never was a time when satirists were more needed to scourge from Parnassus the magpies who are devouring the food scattered there for the singing birds." This scourge she somewhat exercises upon writers who "did not write because they felt obliged to relieve themselves of the swelling thought within, but as an elegant exercise which may win them rank and reputation above the crowd. Their lamp is not lit by the sacred and inevitable lightning from above, but carefully fed by their own will to be seen of men."

These metaphors no longer express the most accepted view of poetical composition. It has been found that those who write chiefly to relieve themselves are very apt to do so at the expense of the reading public. The "inevitable lightning," with which some are stricken, does not lead to such good work as does the "lamp carefully fed" by a steadfast will, whose tenor need not be summarily judged.

These strictures are intended to apply to versifiers in England as well as in America.

"Yet," she says, "there is a middle class, composed of men of little original poetic power, but of much poetic taste and sensibility, whom we would not wish to have silenced. They do no harm, but much good (if only their minds are not confounded with those of a higher class), by educating in others the faculties dominant in themselves." In this class she places Mr. Longfellow, towards whom she confesses "a coolness, in consequence of the exaggerated

praises that have been bestowed upon him."
Perhaps the best thing she says about him is
that "nature with him, whether human or external, is always seen through the windows of
literature."

Mr. Longfellow did, indeed, dwell in the
beautiful house of culture, but with a heart
deeply sensitive to the touch of the humanity
that lay encamped around it. In the "Psalm of
Life," his banner, blood-red with sympathy, was
hung upon the outer wall. And all his further
parley with the world was through the silver
trumpet of peace.

According much praise to William Ellery
Channing, and not a little to Cornelius Mat-
thews, a now almost forgotten writer, Margaret
declares Mr. Lowell to be "absolutely wanting
in the true spirit and tone of poesy." She says
further : —

"His interest in the moral questions of the
day has supplied the want of vitality in himself.
His great facility at versification has enabled
him to fill the ear with a copious stream of
pleasant sound. But his verse is stereotyped,
his thought sounds no depth, and posterity will
not remember him."

The "Biglow Papers" were not yet written,
nor the "Vision of Sir Launfal." Still less was
foreseen the period of the struggle whose victori-

ous close drew from Mr. Lowell a " Commemoration Ode" worthy to stand beside Mr. Emerson's
" Boston Hymn."

In presenting a study of Margaret's thoughts
and life, it seemed to us impossible to omit some
consideration of her pronounced opinions concerning the most widely known of her American
compeers in literature. Having brought these
before the reader, we find it difficult to say the
right word concerning them.

In accepting or rejecting a criticism, we
should consider, first, its intention ; secondly, its
method ; and, in the third place, its standard.
If the first be honorable, the second legitimate,
and the third substantial, we shall adopt the
conclusion arrived at as a just result of analytic
art.

In the judgments just quoted, we must believe
the intention to have been a sincere one. But
neither the method nor the standard satisfies us.
The one is arbitrary, the other unreal. Our
friend's appreciation of her contemporaries was
influenced, at the time of her writing, by idio-
syncrasies of her own which could not give the
law to the general public. These were shown
in her great dislike of the smooth and stereotyped in manner, and her impatience of the
common level of thought and sentiment. The
unusual had for her a great attraction. It prom-

ised originality, which to her seemed a condition of truth itself. She has said in this very paper: " No man can be absolutely true to himself, eschewing cant, compromise, servile imitation, and complaisance, without becoming original."

Here we seem to find a confusion between two conceptions of the word " original." Originality in one acceptation is vital and universal. We originate from the start, and do not *become original.* But the power to develop forms of thought which shall deserve to be called original is a rare gift, and one which even conscience cannot command at will.

The sentences here quoted and commented on show us that Margaret, almost without her own knowledge, was sometimes a partisan of the intellectual reaction of the day, which attacked, in the name of freedom, the fine, insensible tyranny of form and precedent. In its place were temporarily enthroned the spontaneous and passionate. Miracles were expected to follow this change of base, oracles from children, availing philosophies from people who were rebels against all philosophy. Margaret's passionate hopefulness at times carried her within this sphere, where, however, her fine perceptions and love of thorough culture did not allow her to remain.

CHAPTER X.

THE time had now come when Margaret's darling wish was to be fulfilled. An opportunity of
going abroad offered itself under circumstances
which she felt able to accept. On the 1st of
August, 1846, she sailed for Europe in the
"Cambria," then the favorite steamer of the
Cunard line, with Captain Judkins, the most
popular and best known of the company's com-
manders. Her travelling companions were Mr.
and Mrs. Marcus Spring, of Eaglewood, N. J.

She anticipated much from this journey, —
delight, instruction, and the bodily view of a
whole world of beauties which she knew, as yet,
only ideally. Beyond and unguessed lay the

mysteries of fate, from whose depths she was never to emerge in her earthly form.

Margaret already possessed the spirit of all that is most valuable in European culture. She knew the writers of the Old World by study, its brave souls by sympathy, its works of art, more imperfectly, through copies and engravings. The Europe which she carried in her mind was not that which the superficial observer sees with careless eyes, nor could it altogether correspond with that which she, in her careful and thoughtful travel, would discern. But the possession of the European mind was a key destined to unlock for her the true significance of European society.

The voyage was propitious. Arriving in England, Margaret visited the Mechanics' Institute in Liverpool, and found the "Dial" quoted in an address recently given by its director. Sentences from the writings of Charles Sumner and Elihu Burritt adorned the pages of Bradshaw's "Railway Guide," and she was soon called upon to note the wide discrepancy between the views of enlightened Englishmen and the selfish policy of their government, corresponding to the more vulgar passions and ambitions of the people at large.

Passing into the Lake Country, she visited Wordsworth at Ambleside, and found "no

Apollo, flaming with youthful glory, but, instead, a reverend old man, clothed in black, and walking with cautious step along the level garden path." The aged poet, then numbering seventy-six years, "but of a florid, fair old age," showed the visitors his household portraits, his hollyhocks, and his fuchsias. His secluded mode of life, Margaret learned, had so separated him from the living issues of the time, that the needs of the popular heart touched him but remotely. She found him, however, less intolerant than she had feared concerning the repeal of the Corn Laws, a measure upon which public opinion was at the time strongly divided.

In this neighborhood Margaret again saw Miss Martineau, at a new home "presented to her by the gratitude of England for her course of energetic and benevolent effort." Dean Milman, historian and dramatist, was here introduced to Margaret, who describes him as "a specimen of the polished, scholarly man of the world."

Margaret now visited various places of interest in Scotland, and in Edinburgh saw Dr. Andrew Combe, Dr. Chalmers, and De Quincey. Dr. Combe, an eminent authority in various departments of medicine and physiology, was a younger brother of George Combe, the distinguished phrenologist. He had much to say

about his tribulations with the American publishers who had pirated one of his works, but
who refused to print an emended edition of it,
on the ground that the book sold well enough as
it was. Margaret describes Dr. Chalmers as
"half shepherd, half orator, florid, portly, yet of
an intellectually luminous appearance."

De Quincey was of the same age as Wordsworth. Margaret finds his " thoughts and
knowledge " of a character somewhat superseded by the progress of the age. She found
him, not the less, " an admirable narrator, not
rapid, but gliding along like a rivulet through
a green meadow, giving and taking a thousand
little beauties not required to give his story due
relief, but each, in itself, a separate boon." She
admires, too, " his urbanity, so opposed to the
rapid, slang, Vivian-Greyish style current in the
literary conversation of the day."

Among Margaret's meditations in Scotland
was one which she records as " the bootless,
best thoughts I had while looking at the dull
bloodstain and blocked-up secret stair of Holy-
rood, at the ruins of Loch Leven Castle, and
afterwards at Abbotsford, where the picture of
Queen Mary's head, as it lay on the pillow when
severed from the block, hung opposite to a fine
caricature of Queen Elizabeth, dancing high and
disposedly." We give here a part of this medi-
tation : —

"Surely, in all the stern pages of life's account-book there is none on which a more terrible price is exacted for every precious endowment. Her rank and reign only made her powerless to do good, and exposed her to danger. Her talents only served to irritate her foes and disappoint her friends. This most charming of women was the destruction of her lovers. Married three times, she had never any happiness as a wife, but in both the connections of her choice found that she had either never possessed or could not retain, even for a few weeks, the love of the men she had chosen. . . . A mother twice, and of a son and daughter, both the children were brought forth in loneliness and sorrow, and separated from her early, her son educated to hate her, her daughter at once immured in a convent. Add the eighteen years of her imprisonment, and the fact that this foolish, prodigal world, when there was in it one woman fitted by her grace and loveliness to charm all eyes and enliven all fancies, suffered her to be shut up to water with her tears her dull embroidery during the full rose-blossom of her life, and you will hardly get beyond this story for a tragedy, not noble, but pallid and forlorn."

From Edinburgh Margaret and her party made an excursion into the Highlands. The

stage-coach was not yet displaced by the loco-
motive, and Margaret enjoyed, from the top,
the varying aspect of that picturesque region.
Perth, Loch Leven, and Loch Katrine were
visited, and Rowardennan, the place from which
the ascent of Ben Lomond is usually made by
travellers. Margaret attempted this feat with
but one companion, and without a guide, the
people at the inn not having warned her of any
danger in so doing.

The ascent she found delightful. So magnificent was the prospect, that, in remembering it,
she said : " Had that been, as afterwards seemed
likely, the last act of my life, there could not
have been a finer decoration painted on the curtain which was to drop upon it."

The proverbial *facilis descensus* did not here
hold good, and the *revocare gradum* nearly cost
Margaret her life. Beginning to descend at four
in the afternoon, the indistinct path was soon
lost. Margaret's companion left her for a moment in search of it, and could not find her.

" Soon he called to me that he had found it
[the path], and I followed in the direction where
he seemed to be. But I mistook, overshot it,
and saw him no more. In about ten minutes
I became alarmed, and called him many times.
It seems he, on his side, did the same, but the
brow of some hill was between us, and we neither saw nor heard one another."

Margaret now made many attempts to extricate herself from her dangerous situation, and at last attained a point from which she could see the lake, and the inn from which she had started in the morning. But the mountain paths were crossed by watercourses, and hemmed in by bogs. After much climbing up and down, Margaret, already wet, very weary, and thinly clad, saw that she must pass the night on the mountain. The spot at which the light forsook her was of so precipitous a character as to leave her, in the dark, no liberty of movement. Yet she did keep in motion of some sort through the whole of that weary night ; and this, she supposes, saved her life. The stars kept her company for two hours, when the mist fell and hid them. The moon rose late, and was but dimly discernible. At length morning came, and Margaret, starting homeward once more, came upon a company of shepherds, who carried her, exhausted, to the inn, where her distressed friends were waiting for news of her. Such was the extent of the mountain, that a party of twenty men, with dogs, sent in search of the missing one, were not heard by her, and did not hear her voice, which she raised from time to time, hoping to call some one to her rescue. The strength of Margaret's much-abused constitution was made evident by her speedy recovery from the effects of this severe exposure. A fit vigil, this, for one who was about to witness the scenes of 1848. She speaks of the experience as " sublime indeed, a never-to-be-forgotten presentation of stern, serene realities. . . . I had had my grand solitude, my Ossianic visions, and the pleasure of sustaining myself." After visiting Glasgow and Stirling, Margaret and her friends returned to England by Abbotsford and Melrose.

In Birmingham Margaret heard two discourses from George Dawson, then considered a young man of much promise. In Liverpool she had already heard James Martineau, and in London she listened to William Fox. She compares these men with William Henry Channing and Theodore Parker : —

" None of them compare in the symmetrical arrangement of extempore discourse, or in pure eloquence and communication of spiritual beauty, with Channing, nor in fulness and sustained flow with Parker."

Margaret's estimate of Martineau is interesting : —

" Mr. Martineau looks like the over-intellectual, the partially developed man, and his speech confirms this impression. He is sometimes conservative, sometimes reformer, not in the sense of eclecticism, but because his powers and views

12

do not find a true harmony. On the conservative side he is scholarly, acute ; on the other, pathetic, pictorial, generous. He is no prophet and no sage, yet a man full of fine affections and thoughts ; always suggestive, sometimes satisfactory."

Mr. Fox appears to her "the reverse of all this. He is homogeneous in his materials, and harmonious in the results he produces. He has great persuasive power ; it is the persuasive power of a mind warmly engaged in seeking truth for itself."

What a leap did our Margaret now make, from Puritanic New England, Roundhead and Cromwellian in its character, into the very heart of Old England, — into that London which, in those days, and for long years after, might have been called the metropolis of the world! Wonders of many sorts the "province in brick" still contains. Still does it most astonish those who bring to it the most knowledge. But the social wonders which it then could boast have passed away, leaving no equals to take their place.

Charles Dickens was then in full bloom, — Thackeray in full bud. Sydney Smith exercised his keen, discreet wit. Kenyon not only wrote about pink champagne, but dispensed it with many other good things. Rogers entertained with exquisite taste, and showed his art-treasures without ostentation. Tom Moore, like a veteran canary, chirped, but would not sing. Lord Brougham and the Iron Duke were seen in the House of Lords. Carlyle growled and imbibed strong tea at Chelsea. The Queen was in the favor of her youth, with her handsome husband always at her side. The Duchess of Sutherland, a beautiful woman with lovely daughters, kept her state at Stafford House. Lord Houghton was known as Monckton Milnes. The Honorable Mrs. Norton wore her dark hair folded upon her classic head, beneath a circlet of diamonds. A first season in London was then a bewilderment of brilliancy in reputations, beauties, and entertainments. Margaret did not encounter the season, but hoped to do so at a later day. For the moment she consoled herself thus : —

"I am glad I did not at first see all that pomp and parade of wealth and luxury in contrast with the misery — squalid, agonizing, ruffianly — which stares one in the face in every street of London, and hoots at the gates of her palaces a note more ominous than ever was that of owl or raven in the portentous times when empires and races have crumbled and fallen from inward decay."

Margaret expresses the hope that the social

revolution, which to her seemed imminent in England, may be a peaceful one, "which shall destroy nothing except the shocking inhumanity of exclusiveness." She speaks with appreciation of the National and Dulwich Galleries, the British Museum, the Zoölogical Gardens. Among the various establishments of benevolence and reform, she especially mentions a school for poor Italian boys, with which Mazzini had much to do. This illustrious man was already an exile in London, as was the German poet, Freiligrath.

Margaret was an admirer of Joanna Baillie, and considered her and the French Madame Roland as "the best specimens hitherto offered of women of a Roman strength and singleness of mind, adorned by the various culture and capable of the various action opened to them by the progress of the Christian idea."

She thus chronicles her visit to Miss Baillie:

"We found her in her little, calm retreat at Hampstead, surrounded by marks of love and reverence from distinguished and excellent friends. Near her was the sister, older than herself, yet still sprightly and full of active kindness, whose character she has, in one of her last poems, indicated with such a happy mixture of sagacity, humor, and tender pathos, and with so absolute a truth of outline. Although no autograph hunter, I asked for theirs; and when the elder gave hers as 'sister to Joanna Baillie,' it drew a tear from my eye, — a good tear, a genuine pearl, fit homage to that fairest product of the soul of man, humble, disinterested tenderness."

Margaret also visited Miss Berry, the friend of Horace Walpole, long a celebrity, and at that time more than eighty years old. In spite of this, Margaret found her still characterized by the charm, " careless nature or refined art," which had made her a social power once and always.

But of all the notable personages who might have been seen in the London of that time, no one probably interested Margaret so much as did Thomas Carlyle. Her introduction to him was from Mr. Emerson, his friend and correspondent; and it was such as to open to her, more than once, the doors of the retired and reserved house, in which neither time nor money was lavished upon the entertainment of strangers.

Mr. Carlyle's impressions of Margaret have now been given to the world in the published correspondence of Carlyle and Emerson. She had, long before, drawn her portrait of him in one of her letters descriptive of London and its worthies. The candid criticism of both is full of interest, and may here be contrasted. Margaret says : —

" I approached him with more reverence after a little experience of England and Scotland had taught me to appreciate the strength and height of that wall of shams and conventions which he, more than any other man, or thousand men, — indeed, he almost alone, — has begun to throw down. He has torn off the veils from hideous facts ; he has burnt away foolish illusions ; he has touched the rocks, and they have given forth musical answer. Little more was wanting to begin to construct the city ; but that little was wanting, and the work of construction is left to those that come after him. Nay, all attempts of the kind he is the readiest to deride, fearing new shams worse than the old, unable to trust the general action of a thought, and finding no heroic man, no natural king, to represent it and challenge his confidence."

How significant is this phrase, — "unable to trust the general action of a thought." This saving faith in the power of just thought Carlyle, the thinker, had not.

With a reverence, then, not blind, but discriminating, Margaret approached this luminous mind, and saw and heard its possessor thus : —

" Accustomed to the infinite wit and exuberant richness of his writings, his talk is still an amazement and a splendor scarcely to be faced with steady eyes. He does not converse, only harangues. It is the usual misfortune of such marked men that they cannot allow other minds room to breathe and show themselves in their atmosphere, and thus miss the refreshment and instruction which the greatest never cease to need from the experience of the humblest. . . . Carlyle, indeed, is arrogant and overbearing, but in his arrogance there is no littleness or self-love : it is the heroic arrogance of some old Scandinavian conqueror ; it is his nature, and the untamable impulse that has given him power to crush the dragons.

" For the higher kinds of poetry he has no sense, and his talk on that subject is delightfully and gorgeously absurd. . . . He puts out his chin sometimes till it looks like the beak of a bird ; and his eyes flash bright, instinctive meanings, like Jove's bird. Yet he is not calm and grand enough for the eagle : he is more like the falcon, and yet not of gentle blood enough for that either. . . . I cannot speak more nor wiselier of him now ; nor needs it. His works are true to blame and praise him, — the Siegfried of England, great and powerful, if not quite invulnerable, and of a might rather to destroy evil than to legislate for good."

In a letter to Mr. Emerson, Margaret gives some account of her visits at the Carlyle mansion. The second of these was on the occasion

of a dinner-party, at which she met "a witty,
French, flippant sort of a man, author of a History of Philosophy, and now writing a life of
Goethe," presumably George Lewes. Margaret
acknowledges that he told stories admirably, and
that his occasional interruptions of Carlyle's
persistent monologue were welcome. Of this,
her summary is too interesting to be omitted
here : —

"For a couple of hours he was talking about
poetry, and the whole harangue was one eloquent proclamation of the defects in his own
mind. Tennyson wrote in verse because the
schoolmasters had taught him that it was great
to do so ; and had thus, unfortunately, been
turned from the true path for a man. Burns
had, in like manner, been turned from his vocation. Shakespeare had not had the good sense
to see that it would have been better to write
straight on in prose ; and such nonsense which,
though amusing enough at first, he ran to death
after a while. . . . The latter part of the evening,
however, he paid us for this by a series of
sketches, in his finest style of railing and rail-
lery, of modern French literature. All were de-
preciating except that of Béranger. Of him he
spoke with perfect justice, because with hearty
sympathy."

The retirement of the ladies to the drawing-room afforded Margaret an opportunity which she had not yet enjoyed.

"I had afterward some talk with Mrs. Carlyle, whom hitherto I had only seen,—for who can speak while her husband is there? I like her very much; she is full of grace, sweetness, and talent. Her eyes are sad and charming."

Margaret saw the Carlyles only once more.

"They came to pass an evening with us. Unluckily, Mazzini was with us, whose society, when he was there alone, I enjoyed more than any. He is a beauteous and pure music; also, he is a dear friend of Mrs. Carlyle. But his being there gave the conversation a turn to progress and ideal subjects, and Carlyle was fluent in invectives on all our 'rose-water imbecilities.' We all felt distant from him, and Mazzini, after some vain efforts to remonstrate, became very sad. Mrs. Carlyle said to me: 'These are but opinions to Carlyle; but to Mazzini, who has given his all, and helped bring his friends to the scaffold in pursuit of such subjects, it is a matter of life and death.'"

Clearly, Carlyle had not, in Margaret's estimation, the true gospel. She would not bow to the Titanic forces, whether met with in the romances of Sand or in his force-theory. And so, bidding him farewell with great admiration, she passes on, as she says, "more lowly, more willing to be imperfect, since Fate permits such noble creatures, after all, to be only this or that. Carlyle is only a lion."

Carlyle, on his side, writes of her to Mr. Emerson : —

" Margaret is an excellent soul : in real regard with both of us here. Since she went, I have been reading some of her papers in a new Book we have got : greatly superior to all I knew before : in fact, the undeniable utterances (now first undeniable to me) of a truly heroic mind ; altogether unique, so far as I know, among the writing women of this generation ; rare enough, too, God knows, among the writing men. She is very narrow, sometimes, but she is truly high. Honor to Margaret, and more and more good speed to her."

At a later day he sums up his impressions of her in this wise : —

" Such a predetermination to eat this big Universe as her oyster or her egg, and to be absolute empress of all height and glory in it that her heart could conceive, I have not before seen in any human soul. Her ' mountain me,' [1] indeed ; but her courage, too, is high and clear, her chivalrous nobleness *à toute épreuve.*"

Margaret's high estimate of Mazzini will be

---

[1] Quoted from Mr. Emerson's reminiscences.

justified by those who knew him or knew of him : —

"Mazzini, one of these noble refugees, is not only one of the heroic, the courageous, and the faithful, — Italy boasts many such, — but he is also one of the wise, — one of those who, disappointed in the outward results of their undertakings, can yet 'bate no jot of heart and hope,' but must 'steer right onward.' For it was no superficial enthusiasm, no impatient energies; that impelled him, but an understanding of what must be the designs of Heaven with regard to man, since God is Love, is Justice. He is one of those beings who, measuring all things by the ideal standard, have yet no time to mourn over failure or imperfection ; there is too much to be done to obviate it."

She finds in his papers, published in the "People's Journal," "the purity of impulse, largeness and steadiness of view, and fineness of discrimination which must belong to a legislator for a *Christian* commonwealth."

Much as Margaret admired the noble sentiments expressed in Mazzini's writings, she admired still more the love and wisdom which led the eminent patriot to found, with others, the school for poor Italian boys already spoken of. More Christ-like did she deem this labor than aught that he could have said or sung.

" As among the fishermen and poor people of Judæa were picked up those who have become to modern Europe a leaven that leavens the whole mass, so may these poor Italian boys yet become more efficacious as missionaries to their people than would an Orphic poet at this period."

At the distribution of prizes to the school, in which Mazzini and Mariotti took part, some of the Polish exiles also being present, she seemed to see " a planting of the kingdom of Heaven."

Margaret saw a good deal of James Garth Wilkinson, who later became prominent as the author of the work entitled " The Human Body in its Relation to the Constitution of Man." She found in him " a sane, strong, and well-exercised mind, but in the last degree unpoetical in its structure." Dr. Wilkinson published, years after this time, a volume of verses which amply sustains this judgment.

" Browning," she writes, " has just married Miss Barrett, and gone to Italy. I may meet them there." Hoping for a much longer visit at some future time, and bewildered, as she says, both by the treasures which she had found, and those which she had not had opportunity to explore, Margaret left London for its social and æsthetic antithesis, Paris.

CHAPTER XI.

IF the aspect of London society has changed
greatly since Margaret's visit there in 1846, the
Paris which she saw that winter may be said to
exist no longer, so completely is its physiognomy
transformed by the events of the last thirty-seven
years. Like London, Paris had then some gems
of the first water, to which nothing in the present day corresponds. Rachel was then queen of
its tragic stage, George Sand supreme in its literary domain. De Balzac, Eugène Sue, Dumás
père, and Béranger then lived and moved among
admiring friends. Victor Hugo was in early
middle age. Guizot was in his full prestige, literary and administrative. Liszt and Chopin held
the opposite poles of the musical world, and

wielded, the one its most intense, the other its broadest power. The civilized world then looked to Paris for the precious traditions of good taste, and the city deserved this deference as it does not now.

The sense of security which then prevailed in the French capital was indeed illusory. The stable basis of things was already undermined by the dangerous action of theories and of thinkers. Louis Philippe was unconsciously nearing the abrupt close of his reign. A new chaos was imminent, and one out of which was to come, first a heroic uprising, and then a despotism so monstrous and mischievous as to foredoom itself, a caricature of military empire which for a time cheated Europe, and in the end died of the emptiness of its own corruption.

Into this Paris Margaret came, not unannounced. Her essay on American Literature, which had recently appeared in her volume entitled "Papers on Literature and Art," had already been translated into French, and printed in the "Revue Indépendante." The same periodical soon after published a notice of "Woman in the Nineteenth Century." Margaret enjoyed the comfortable aspect of the apartment which she occupied with her travelling-companions at Hôtel Rougemont, Boulevard Poissoniere. She mentions the clock, mirror, curtained bed, and

small wood-fire which were then, and are to-day,
so costly to the transient occupant.

Though at first not familiar with the sound of
the French language, she soon had some pleasant acquaintances, and was not long in finding
her way to the literary and social eminences who
were prepared to receive her as their peer.

First among these she mentions George Sand,
to whom she wrote a letter, calling afterwards
at her house. Her name was not rightly re-
ported by the peasant woman who opened the
door, and Margaret, waiting for admittance,
heard at first the discouraging words, " Madame
says she does not know you." She stopped to
send a message regarding the letter she had
written, and as she spoke, Madame Sand
opened the door and stood looking at her for
a moment.

" Our eyes met. I shall never forget her look
at that moment. The doorway made a frame
for her figure. She is large, but well formed.
She was dressed in a robe of dark violet silk,
with a black mantle on her shoulders, her beautiful hair dressed with the greatest taste, her
whole appearance and attitude, in its simple and
lady-like dignity, presenting an almost ludicrous
contrast to the vulgar caricature idea of George
Sand. Her face is a very little like the portraits,
but much finer. The upper part of the forehead

and eyes are beautiful, the lower strong and
masculine, expressive of a hardy temperament
and strong passions, but not in the least coarse,
the complexion olive, and the air of the whole
head Spanish." This striking apparition was
further commended in Margaret's eyes by " the
expression of goodness, nobleness, and power "
that characterized the countenance of the great
French-woman.

Madame Sand said, " C'est vous," and offered
her hand to Margaret, who, taking it, answered,
" Il me fait du bien de vous voir " (" It does me
good to see you "). They went into the study.
Madame Sand spoke of Margaret's letter as
charmante, and the two ladies then talked on
for hours, as if they had always known each
other. Madame Sand had at that moment a
work in the press, and was hurried for copy,
and beset by friends and visitors. She kept
all these at a distance, saying to Margaret : " It
is better to throw things aside, and seize the
present moment." Margaret gives this *résumé*
of the interview : " We did not talk at all of personal or private matters. I saw, as one sees in
her writings, the want of an independent, interior
life, but I did not feel it as a fault. I heartily
enjoyed the sense of so rich, so prolific, so ardent a genius. I liked the woman in her, too,
very much ; I never liked a woman better."

To complete the portrait, Margaret mentions the cigarette, which her new friend did not relinquish during the interview. The impression received as to character did not materially differ from that already made by her writings. In seeing her, Margaret was not led to believe that all her mistakes were chargeable upon the unsettled condition of modern society. Yet she felt not the less convinced of the generosity and nobleness of her nature. "There may have been something of the Bacchante in her life," says Margaret, some reverting to the wild ecstasies of heathen nature-worship, "but she was never coarse, never gross."

Margaret saw Madame Sand a second time, surrounded by her friends, and with her daughter, who was then on the eve of her marriage with the sculptor Clésinger. In this *entourage* she had "the position of an intellectual woman and good friend; the same as my own," says Margaret, "in the circle of my acquaintance as distinguished from my intimates."

Beneath the same roof Margaret found Chopin, "always ill, and as frail as a snow-drop, but an exquisite genius. He played to me, and I liked his talking scarcely less." The Polish poet, Mickiewicz, said to her, "Chopin gives us the Ariel view of the universe."

Margaret had done her best while in London to see what the English stage had to offer. The result had greatly disappointed her. In France she found the theatre living, and found also a public which would not have tolerated "one touch of that stage-strut and vulgar bombast of tone which the English actor fancies indispensable to scenic illusion."

In Paris she says that she saw, for the first time, "something represented in a style uniformly good." Besides this general excellence, which is still aimed at in the best theatres of the Continent, the Parisian stage had then a star of the first magnitude, whose splendor was without an equal, and whose setting brought no successor. In the supreme domain of tragic art, Rachel then reigned, an undisputed queen. Like George Sand, her brilliant front was obscured by the cloud of doubt which rested upon her private character, — a matter of which even the most dissolute age will take note, after its fashion. And yet the charmed barrier of the footlights surrounded her with a flame of mystery. Whatever was known or surmised of her elsewhere, within those limits she appeared as the living impersonation of beauty, grace, and power. For Rachel had, at this time, no public sorrow. How it might fare with her and her lovers little concerned the crowds who gathered nightly, drawn by the lightnings of her eye, the melodious thunder of her voice. Ten years later, a new favorite, her rival but not her equal, came to win the heart of her Paris from her. Then Rachel, grieved and angry, knew the vanity of all human dependence. She crossed the ocean, and gave the New World a new delight. But in spite of its laurels and applause, she sickened (Margaret had said she could not live long), and fled far, far eastward, to hear in ancient Egypt the death-psalms of her people. With a smile, the last change of that expressive countenance, its lovely light expired.

Of the woman, Margaret says nothing. Of the artist, she says that she found her worthy of Greece, and fit to be made immortal in its marble. She did not, it is true, find in her the most tender pathos, nor yet the sublime of sweetness : —

"Her range, even in high tragedy, is limited. Her noblest aspect is when sometimes she expresses truth in some severe shape, and rises, simple and austere, above the mixed elements around her." Had Margaret seen her in "Les Horaces"? One would think so.

"On the dark side, she is very great in hatred and revenge. I admired her more in Phèdre than in any other part in which I saw her. The guilty love inspired by the hatred of a goddess was expressed with a force and terrible naturalness that almost suffocated the beholder."

Margaret had heard much about the power which Rachel could throw into a single look, and speaks of it as indeed magnificent. Yet she admired most in her " the grandeur, truth, and depth of her conception of each part, and the sustained purity with which she represented it."

In seeing other notabilities, Margaret was indeed fortunate. She went one day to call upon Lamennais, to whom she brought a letter of introduction. To her disappointment, she found him not alone. But the " citizen-looking, vivacious, elderly man," whom she was at first sorry to see with him, turned out to be the poet Béranger, and Margaret says that she was " very happy in that little study, in presence of these two men whose influence has been so great, so real." It was indeed a very white stone that hit two such birds at one throw.

Margaret heard a lecture from Arago, and was not disappointed in him. " Clear, rapid, full, and equal was this discourse, and worthy of the master's celebrity."

The Chamber of Deputies was in those days much occupied with the Spanish Marriage, as it was called. This was the intended betrothal of

the Queen of Spain's sister to the Duc de Mont-
pensier, youngest son of the then reigning King
of the French, Louis Philippe. Guizot and
Thiers were both heard on this matter, but Margaret heard only M. Berryer, then considered
the most eloquent speaker of the House. His
oratory appeared to her, " indeed, very good ; not
logical, but plausible, with occasional bursts of
flame and showers of sparks." While admiring him, Margaret thinks that her own country
possesses public speakers of more force, and of
equal polish.

At a presentation and ball at the Tuileries
Margaret was much struck with the elegance
and grace of the Parisian ladies of high society.
The Queen made the circuit of state, with the
youthful Duchess, the cause of so much dis-
turbance, hanging on her arm. Margaret found
here some of her own country women, conspicuous for their beauty. The uniforms and decorations of the gentlemen contrasted favorably, in
her view, with the sombre, black-coated masses
of men seen in circles at home.

"Among the crowd wandered Leverrier, in
the costume of an Academician, looking as if he
had lost, not found, his planet. He seemed not
to find it easy to exchange the music of the
spheres for the music of fiddles."

The Italian Opera in Paris fell far short of

Margaret's anticipations. So curtly does she judge it, that one wonders whether she expected to find it a true Parnassus, dedicated to the ideal expression of the most delicate and lofty sentiment. Grisi appeared to her coarse and shallow, Persiani mechanical and meretricious, Mario devoid of power. Lablache alone satisfied her.

These judgments show something of the weakness of off-hand criticism. In the world of art, the critic who wishes to teach, must first be taught of the artist. He must be very sure that he knows what a work of art is before he carps at what it is not. Relying on her own great intelligence, and on her love of beautiful things, Margaret expected, perhaps, to understand too easily the merits and defects of what she saw and heard.

In Paris Margaret met Alexandre Vattemare, intent upon his project of the exchange of superfluous books and documents between the public libraries of different countries. Busy as he was, he found time to be of service to her, and it was through his efforts that she was enabled to visit the Imprimerie Royale and the Mint. He also induced the Librarian of the Chamber of Deputies to show her the manuscripts of Rousseau, which she found "just as he has celebrated them, written on fine white paper, tied with ribbon. Yellow and faded, age has made them," says Margaret ; "yet at their touch I seemed to feel the fire of youth, immortally glowing, more and more expansive, with which his soul has pervaded this century."

M. Vattemare introduced Margaret to one of the evening schools of the Frères Chrétiens, where she saw with pleasure how much can be accomplished for the working classes by evening lessons.

"Visions arose in my mind of all that might be done in our country by associations of men and women who have received the benefits of literary culture, giving such evening lessons throughout our cities and villages." Margaret wishes, however, that such disinterested effort in our own country should not be accompanied by the priestly robe and manner which for her marred the humanity of the Christian Brotherhood of Paris.

The establishment of the Protestant Deaconesses is praised by Margaret. She visited also the School for Idiots, near Paris, where her feelings vented themselves in "a shower of sweet and bitter tears ; of joy at what has been done, of grief for all that I and others possess, and cannot impart to these little ones." She was much impressed with the character of the master of the school, a man of seven or eight and twenty years, whose fine countenance she saw "looking in love on those distorted and opaque vases of humanity."

Turning her face southward, she thus takes leave of the great capital: —

"Paris! I was sad to leave thee, thou wonderful focus, where ignorance ceases to be a pain, because there we find such means daily. to lessen it."

Railroads were few in the France of forty years ago. Margaret came by diligence and boat to Lyons, to Avignon, where she waded through the snow to visit the tomb of Laura, and to Marseilles, where she embarked for Genoa. Her first sight of this city did not disappoint her, but to her surprise, she found the weather cold and ungenial: —

"I could not realize that I had actually touched those shores to which I had looked forward all my life, where it seemed that the heart would expand, and the whole nature be turned to delight. Seen by a cutting wind, the marble palaces, the gardens, the magnificent water-view, failed to charm." Both here and in Leghorn Margaret visited Italians at their houses, and found them very attractive, "charming women, refined and eloquent men." The Mediterranean voyage was extended as far as Naples, which she characterizes as "priest-ridden, misgoverned, full of dirty, degraded men and women, yet still most lovely." And here, after a week which appeared to be "an exact copy of the miseries of a New-England spring," with a wind "villanous, horrible, exactly like the worst east wind of Boston," Margaret found at last her own Italy, and found it "beautiful, worthy to be loved and embraced, not talked about. . . . Baiæ had still a hid divinity for me, Vesuvius a fresh baptism of fire; and Sorrento — oh! Sorrento was beyond picture, beyond poesy."

After Naples came Margaret's first view of Rome, where she probably arrived early in May, and where she remained until late in the month of June. We do not find among her letters of this period any record of her first impressions of the Eternal City, the approach to which, before the days of railroads in Italy, was unspeakably impressive and solemn.

Seated in the midst of her seven hills, with the desolate Campagna about her, one could hardly say whether her stony countenance invited the spirit of the age, or defied it. Her mediæval armor was complete at all points. Her heathen heart had kept Christianity far from it by using as exorcisms the very forms which, at the birth of that religion, had mediated between its spirit and the dull sense of the Pagan world. It was the nineteenth century in America, the eighteenth in England, the seventeenth in France, and the fifteenth in Rome. The aged hands of the grandam still held fast the key of her treasures. Her haughty front still said to Ruin and Desolation, —

"Here is my throne, bid kings come bow to it."

So the writer first saw Rome in the winter of 1843. Her walls seemed those of a mighty sepulchre, in which even the new-born babe was born into death. The stagnation of thought, the prohibition of question, the denial of progress! Her ministers had a sweet Lethean draught with which to lull the first clamors of awakening life, to quiet the first promptings of individual thought. It was the draught of Circe, fragrant but fatal. And those who fed upon it became pathetic caricatures of humanity.

Not so did Margaret find Rome in 1847. The intervening years had wrought a change. Within the defiant fortress of superstition a divine accident had happened. A man had been brought to the chair of St. Peter who felt his own human power too strongly to consent to the impotence of the traditional *non possumus*. To the timid questioning of Freedom from without he gave the bold answer of Freedom from within. The Papal crown had sometimes covered the brows of honest, heroic men. Such an one would he prove himself, and his first message was to that effect. Fortunate, fatal error ! The thrones of the earth trembled at it. Crowned heads shook with the palsy of fear. The enslaved multitudes and their despised champions sent up a ringing shout to heaven, for the apocalyptic hour had come. The sixth seal was broken, and the cannon of St. Angelo, which saluted the crowning of the new Pontiff, really saluted the installation of the new era.

Alas ! many woes had to intervene before this new order could establish itself upon any permanent foundation. The Pope forsook his lofty ground. France, republican for a day only, became the ally of absolutism, and sent an army to subdue those who had believed the papal promise and her own. After a frightful interval of suffering and resistance, this was effected, and Pius was brought back, shorn of his splendors, a Jove whose thunderbolt had been stolen, a man without an idea. Then came the confusion of endless doubt and question. What had been the secret of the Pope's early liberalism ? What that of his *volte-face ?* Was it true, as was afterwards maintained, that he had been, from the first, a puppet, moved by forces quite outside his own understanding, and that the moving hands, not the puppet, had changed ? Or had he gone to war with mighty Precedent, without counting the cost of the struggle, and so failed? Or had he undergone a poisoning which broke his spirit and touched his brain?

These were the questions of that time, not ours to answer, brought to mind here only because they belong to the history of Margaret's years in Italy, years in which she learned to love that country as her own, and to regard it as the land of her spiritual belonging.

CHAPTER XII.

IN this first visit to Rome, Margaret could not avoid some touch of the disenchantment which usually comes with the experience of what has been long and fondly anticipated. She had soon seen all that is preserved of "the fragments of the great time," and says: "They are many and precious; yet is there not so much of high excellence as I looked for. They will not float the heart on a boundless sea of feeling, like the starry night on our Western prairies." She confesses herself more interested at this moment in the condition and prospects of the Italian people than in works of art, ancient or modern. In spite of this, she seems to have been diligent in visiting the galleries and studios of Rome. Among the latter she mentions those of the sculptors Macdonald, Wolff, Tenerani, and Gott, whose groups of young people and animals were to her "very refreshing after the grander attempts of the present time." She found our own Crawford just completing a bust of his beautiful wife, which is to-day a household treasure among her relatives. Margaret preferred his designs to those of Gibson, who was then considered the first of English sculptors. Among American painters she found Terry, Cranch, and Hicks at work. She saw the German Overbeck surrounded by his pictures, looking "as if he had just stepped out of one of them, — a lay monk, with a pious eye, and habitual morality of thought which limits every gesture."

Among the old masters, Domenichino and Titian were those whom she learned to appreciate only by the actual sight of their paintings. Other artists, she thinks, may be well understood through copies and engravings, but not these. She enjoyed the frescos of Caracci with " the purest pleasure," tired soon of Guercino, who had been one of her favorites, and could not like Leonardo da Vinci at all. His pictures, she confesses, "show a wonderful deal of study and thought. I hate to see the marks of them. I want a simple and direct expression of soul." For the explanation of these remarks we must refer the reader back to what Mr. Emerson has said of Margaret's idiosyncratic mode of judgment. Raphael and Michael Angelo were already so well known to her through engravings, that their paintings and frescos made no new impression upon her. Not so was it with Michael's sculptures. Of his Moses she says: "It is the only thing in Europe so far which has entirely outgone my hopes."

But the time was not one in which an enthusiast like Margaret could be content to withdraw from living issues into the calm impersonality of art. The popular life around her was throbbing with hopes and excitements to which it had long been unaccustomed. Visions of a living Italy flashed through the crevices of a stony despair which had lasted for ages. The prospect of representative government was held out to the Roman people, and the promise was welcomed by a torchlight procession which streamed through the Corso like a river of fire, and surging up to the Quirinal, where Pius then dwelt, "made it a mound of light." The noble Greek figures were illuminated, and their calm aspect contrasted strongly with the animated faces of the Italians. "The Pope appeared on his balcony; the crowd shouted their *vivas*. He extended his arms, the crowd fell on their knees and received his benediction." Margaret says that she had never seen anything finer.

In this new enthusiasm the people agreed to celebrate the birthday of Rome.

"A great dinner was given at the Baths of Titus, in the open air. The company was on the grass in the area, the music at one end; boxes filled with the handsome Roman women occupied the other sides. It was a new thing here, this popular dinner, and the Romans greeted it in an intoxication of hope and pleasure." Many political exiles, amnestied by the Pope, were present. The Marquis d' Azeglio, painter, novelist, and diplomatist, was the most noted of the speakers. From this renewed, regenerated Rome Margaret went on to visit the northern cities of Italy, passing through Perugia on her way to Florence. In this neighborhood she explored the churches of Assisi, and the Etruscan tombs, then newly discovered. She was enchanted with the beauty of Perugia, its noble situation, and its treasures of early art. Florence interested her less than "cities more purely Italian. The natural character is ironed out here, and done up in a French pattern; yet there is no French vivacity, nor Italian either." The Grand Duke was at the time in an impossible position between his allegiance to the liberalizing Pope and his fealty to despotic Austria. Tuscany accordingly was "glum as death" on the outside, but glowing with dangerous fire within.

Margaret, before leaving Florence, wrote: "Florence is not like Rome. At first I could not bear the change; yet, for the study of the fine arts, it is a still richer place. Worlds of thought have risen in my mind; some time you will have light from all."

Here she visited the studios of her countrymen, Horatio Greenough and Hiram Powers, and, after a month's stay, went on to Bologna, where she greatly appreciated the truly Italian physiognomy of the city, and rejoiced in the record of its women artists and professors, nobly recognized and upheld by their fellow-citizens.

Thence she went to Ravenna, prized for its curious remains, its Byronic memories, and its famous Pineta, dear to students of Dante. After this came a fortnight in Venice, which, like Angelo's Moses, surpassed her utmost expectations: "There only I began to feel in its fulness Venetian art. It can only be seen in its own atmosphere. Never had I the least idea of what is to be seen at Venice."

The city was, in those days, a place of refuge for throneless royalty. The Duchesse de Berri and her son had each a palace on the Grand

Canal. A queen of another sort, Taglioni, here consoled herself for the quiet of her retirement from the stage. Margaret had the pleasure of an outside view of the *fête* given by the royal Duchess in commemoration of her son's birthday. The aged Duchesse d'Angoulème came from Vienna to be present on the occasion.

" 'T was a scene of fairy-land, the palace full of light, so that from the canal could be seen even the pictures on the walls. Landing from the gondolas, the elegantly dressed ladies and gentlemen seemed to rise from the water. We also saw them glide up the great stair, rustling their plumes, and in the reception-room make and receive the customary grimaces." A fine band of music completed the attractions of the scene. Margaret, listening and looking hard by, " thought of the Stuarts, Bourbons, and Bonapartes in Italy, and offered up a prayer that other names might be added to the list, and other princes, more rich in blood than in brain, might come to enjoy a perpetual *villeggiatura* in Italy."

From Venice Margaret journeyed on to Milan, stopping on the way at Vicenza, Verona, Mantua, Lago di Garda, and Brescia. These ten days of travel opened to her long vistas of historic study, delightful to contemplate, even if hopeless to explore fully. No ten days of her previous life, she is sure, ever brought her so far in this direction. In approaching Milan her thoughts reverted to the "Promessi Sposi." Nearly asleep for a moment, she heard the sound of waters, and started up to ask, "Is that the Adda?" She had guessed rightly. The authorship of this classic work seemed to her to secure to its writer, Manzoni, the right of eminent domain in and around Milan. Writing to Mr. Emerson from this city, she says:—

"To-day, for the first time, I have seen Manzoni. Manzoni has spiritual efficacy in his looks; his eyes still glow with delicate tenderness. His manners are very engaging, frank, expansive; every word betokens the habitual elevation of his thoughts, and (what *you* care for so much) he says distinct, good things. He lives in the house of his fathers, in the simplest manner."

Manzoni had, at the time, somewhat displeased his neighbors by a second marriage, scarcely considered suitable for him. Margaret, however, liked the new wife very well, "and saw why he married her."

She found less to see in Milan than in other Italian cities, and was glad to have there some days of quiet after the fatigues of her journey, which had been augmented at Brescia by a brief attack of fever. She mentions with interest the bust of the celebrated mathematician, Maria Gaetana Agnesi, preserved in the Ambrosian Library. Among her new acquaintances here were some young Italian radicals, "interested in ideas."

The Italian Lakes and Switzerland came next in the order of her travels. Her Swiss tour she calls " a little romance by itself," promising to give, at a later date, a description of it, which we fail to find anywhere. Returning from it, she passed a fortnight at Como, and saw something of the Italian nobility, who pass their summers on its shores. Here she enjoyed the society of the accomplished Marchesa Arconati Visconti, whom she had already met in Florence, and who became to her a constant and valued friend.

Margaret found no exaggeration in the enthusiasm expressed by poets and artists for the scenery of this lake region. The descriptions of it given by Goethe, Richter, and Taylor had not prepared her for what she saw. Even Turner's pictures had fallen short of the real beauty. At Lugano she met Lady Franklin, the widow of the Arctic explorer. She returned to Milan by the 8th of September, in time for the great feast of the Madonna, and finally left the city " with great regret, and hope to return." In a letter to her brother Richard she speaks of her radical friends there as "a circle of aspiring youth, such as I have not known in any other city." Conspicuous among these was the young Marquis Guerrieri Gonzaga, commended to her by "a noble soul, the quietest sensibility, and a brilliant and ardent, though not a great, mind." This gentleman has to-day a recognized position in Italy as a thoroughly enlightened and intelligent liberal.

Margaret found among the Milanese, as she must have anticipated, a great hatred of the Austrian rule, aggravated, at the time of her second visit, by acts of foolish and useless repression. On the occasion of the festivals attending the entry of a new archbishop, some youths (among them possibly Margaret's radical friends) determined to sing the hymn composed at Rome in honor of Pius IX. The consequence of this was a charge of the armed Austrian police upon the defenceless crowd of people present, who, giving way, were stabbed by them in the back. Margaret's grief and indignation at this state of things made her feel keenly the general indifference of her own travelling country-people to the condition and fate of Italy.

"Persons who call themselves Americans, — miserable, thoughtless Esaus, unworthy their high birthright . . . absorbed at home by the lust of gain, the love of show, abroad, they see only the equipages, the fine clothes, the food. They have no heart for the idea, for the destiny of our own great nation : how can they feel the spirit that is struggling in this ? "

The condition of Italy has been greatly altered for the better since Margaret wrote these words, thirty-six years ago ; but the American traveller of this type is to-day, to all intents and purposes, what he was then.

Margaret left Milan before the end of this September, to return to Rome. She explored with delight the great Certosa of Pavia, and in Parma saw the Correggio pictures, of which she says : "A wonderful beauty it is that informs them, — not that which is the chosen food of my soul, yet a noble beauty, and which did its message to me also." Parma and Modena appear to her " obliged to hold their breath while their poor, ignorant sovereigns skulk in corners, hoping to hide from the coming storm."

Before reaching Rome, Margaret made a second visit to Florence. The liberty of the press had been recently established in Tuscany, under happy auspices. This freedom took effect in the establishment of two liberal papers, "Alba " ("The Dawn "), and "Patria," needless to translate. The aim of these was to educate the youth and the working classes, by promoting fearlessness in thought and temperance in action.

The creation of the National Guard had given confidence to the people. Shortly before Margaret's arrival this event had been celebrated by a grand public festival, preceded by a general reconciliation of public and private differences, and culminating in a general embracing, and exchanging of banners. She speaks of this as a "new great covenant of brotherly love," in which "all was done in that beautiful poetic manner peculiar to this artist-people." In this feast of reconciliation resident Americans bore their part, Horatio Greenough taking the lead among them. Margaret's ears were refreshed by continually hearing in the streets the singing of the Roman hymn composed in honor of Pope Pius. Wishing that her own country might send some substantial token of sympathy to the land of its great discoverers, she suggests that a cannon, named for one of these, would be the most fitting gift.[1] The first letter from Rome after these days is dated Oct. 18, 1847.

[1] Cabot, a well-known Boston patronymic.

CHAPTER XIII.

THE period in which Margaret now found herself, and its circumstances, may best be described by the adjective "billowy." Up and
down, up and down, went the hearts and hopes
of the liberal party. Hither and thither ran
the tides of popular affection, suspicion, and resentment. The Pope was the idol of the moment. Whoever might do wrong, he could not.
The Grand Duke of Tuscany, described by Margaret as dull but well meaning, yielded to pressure wherever it became most severe. The
Austrian occupation was cowardly and cruel, as
ever. The minor princes, who had been from

their birth incapable of an idea, tried as well as they could to put on some semblance of concession without really yielding anything.

The King of Sardinia was spoken of among the liberals as a worthless man, without heart or honor, only likely to be kept on the right side by the stress of circumstance. This judgment of him was reversed in after years, when, behind Casa Guidi windows, Elizabeth Barrett Browning wrote, with steadfast hand, " Yea, verily, Charles Albert has died well."

The royalty of Naples tried to quiet its tremors with blood, and trembled still. And in the midst of all this turmoil, down comes Louis Philippe from his throne, and France is shaken to her very centre.

To follow Margaret through all the fluctuations and excitements consequent upon these events would be no easy task. She was obviously in close relations with leading Italian liberals, and probably trusted their statements and shared their hopes, fears, and resentments. Constant always in her faith in human nature, and in her zeal for the emancipation of Italy, the dissolving view before her could leave her no other fixed belief. Her favorites, her beloved Italian people, even her adored Rome, appeared to her at different times in very various lights.

Starting from the date given above, we will

follow, as well as we can, her progress through
the constantly shifting scenes that surrounded
her, from whose intense interest she could not,
for one moment, isolate herself.

Of her return to Rome, Margaret says: " All
mean things were forgotten in the joy that
rushed over me like a flood." The difference
between a sight-seeing tour and a winter's residence in such a place is indeed like that between
a chance acquaintance and an intimate one.
Settled in a pleasant apartment on the Corso,
"in a house of loving Italians," Margaret promised herself a winter of "tranquil companionship" with what she calls " the true Rome."

She did not find the Italian autumn beautiful,
as she had expected, but she enjoyed the Octo-
ber *festas* of the Trasteverini, and went with
" half Rome ' to see the manœuvres of the Civic
Guard on the Campagna, near the tomb of
Cecilia Metella.

To the music of the "Bolognese March" six
thousand Romans moved in battle array, in full
sight of the grandiose débris of the heroic time.

Some sight-seeing Margaret still undertook,
as we learn from a letter dated November 17, in
which she speaks of going about "in a coach
with several people," and confesses that she dis-
sipates her thoughts on outward beauty. Such

was her delight, at this time, in the "atmosphere of the European mind," that she even
wished, for a time, to be delivered from the
sound of the English language.

The beginning of this winter was, as it usually
is in Italy, a season of fine weather. On the 17th
of December Margaret rises to bask in beneficent
floods of sunlight, and to find upon her table the
roses and grapes which, in New England, would
have been costly hot-house luxuries. Her letter of this date is full of her delight in having
penetrated from the outer aspect to the heart
of Rome, classic, mediæval, and modern. And
here we come upon the record of those first
impressions concerning which we latterly indulged in some speculation.

"Ah ! how joyful to see once more this
Rome, instead of the pitiful, peddling, Anglicized
Rome first viewed in unutterable dismay from the
coupé of the vettura, — a Rome all full of taverns,
lodging-houses, cheating chambermaids, vilest
valets de place, and fleas ! A Niobe of nations
indeed ! Ah ! why (secretly the heart blas-
phemed) did the sun omit to kill her too, when
all the glorious race which wore her crown fell
beneath his ray ?"

All this had now disappeared for Margaret,
and a new enchantment had taken the place of
the old illusion and disappointment. For she

was now able to disentangle the strange jumble
of ancient and modern Rome. In this more
understanding and familiar view, she says : —

"The old kings, the consuls and tribunes, the
emperors, drunk with blood and gold, return for
us. The seven hills tower, the innumerable
temples glitter, and the Via Sacra swarms with
triumphal life once more."

In the later Papal Rome she discerns, through
the confusion of rite and legend, a sense which
to her marks the growth "of the human spirit
struggling to develop its life." And the Rome
of that day was dear to her in spite of its manifold corruptions ; dear for the splendor of the
race, surviving every enslaving and deforming
influence ; dear for the new-born hope of freedom which she considered safe in the nursing
of Pope Pius.

Most of the occasions chronicled by Margaret
in her letters of this period are of the sort
familiarly known to travellers, and even to readers of books of travel.

The prayers for the dead, early in November,
the festival of San Carlo Borromeo, the veiling
of a nun, the worship of the wooden image
called "the most Holy Child," idolatrous, Margaret thinks, as that of the Capitoline Jove, the
blessing of the animals, the festival of the Magi
at the Propaganda, — these events are all de-

scribed by her with much good thought and suggestion.

She saw the Pope occasionally at the grand ceremonies of the Church, and saw the first shadow fall upon his popularity, partly in consequence of some public utterances of his which seemed to Margaret " deplorably weak in thought and absolute in manner," and which she could not but interpret as implying that wherever reform might in future militate against sacerdotal traditions, it would go to the wall, in order that the priest might triumph.

The glorious weather had departed almost as soon as she had sung its praises, namely, on the 18th of December ; after which time her patience was sorely tried by forty days of rain, accompanied by "abominable reeking odors, such as blessed cities swept by the sea-breeze never know." We copy from one of her letters a graphic picture of this time of trial : —

" It has been dark all day, though the lamp has only been lit half an hour. The music of the day has been, first, the atrocious *arias* which last in the Corso till near noon. Then came the wicked organ-grinder, who, apart from the horror of the noise, grinds exactly the same obsolete abominations as at home or in England, the 'Copenhagen Waltz,' 'Home, Sweet Home,' and all that ! The cruel chance that both an

English my-lady and a councillor from the prov-
inces live opposite, keeps him constantly before
my window, hoping for *bajocchi*.

" Within, the three pet dogs of my landlady,
bereft of their walk, unable to employ their
miserable legs and eyes, exercise themselves by
a continual barking, which is answered by all
the dogs in the neighborhood. An urchin returning from the laundress, delighted with the
symphony, lays down his white bundle in the
gutter, seats himself on the curb-stone, and attempts an imitation of the music of cats as a
tribute to the concert.

" The door-bell rings. *Chi è?* ('Who is it?')
cries the handmaid. Enter a man poisoning me
at once with the smell of the worst possible cigars,
insisting I shall look upon frightful, ill-cut cam-
eos and worse-designed mosaics, made by some
friend of his. Man of ill odors and meanest
smile! I am no countess to be fooled by you."

These passages give us some glimpses of our
friend in the surroundings which at first gave
her so much satisfaction, and whose growing
discomforts were lightened for her by her native
sense of humor.

In spite of this, however, " the dirt, the gloom,
the desolation of Rome" affected her severely.
Her appetite failed, and with it her strength,
while nervous headache and fever conspired to

make the whole season appear, in review, " the most idle and most suffering " one of her life.

The most important public event of the winter in Rome seems to have been the inauguration of a new Council, with some show of popular election, said to have been on the whole satisfactory. As this was considered a decided step in the direction of progress, preparations were made for its celebration by the representatives of other Italian States, and of various friendly nations. The Americans resident in Rome were aroused to an unwonted degree of interest, the gentlemen subscribing funds for the materials of a flag, and the ladies meeting to make it. To accompany this banner, a magnificent spread eagle was procured. Everything was in the height of preparation, when some counter-influence, brought to bear upon the Pope, led him to issue an edict forbidding this happy concourse of the flags of all nations, and allowing only that of Rome to be carried in honor of the occasion. Margaret saw in this the work of the Oscurantists, " ever on the watch to do mischief" to the popular cause.

Despite the disappointment of the citizens at this curtailment of their show, the streets were decorated, and filled with people in the best humor. Margaret was able to see nothing but this crowd, but found even that a great pleasure. A ball at the Argentina Theatre terminated the festivities of the day. Here were seen " Lord Minto; Prince Corsini, now senator; the Torlonias, in uniform of the Civic Guard, Princess Torlonia (the beautiful Colonna) in a sash of their colors, which she waved often in answer to their greetings." The finest show of the evening, Margaret says, was the native Saltarello, danced by the Trasteverini in their gayest costumes. In this dance, which is at once very *naïve* and very natural, Margaret saw the embodiment of " the Italian wine, the Italian sun."

In the course of this winter it became evident that the liberalism of Pio Nono would not stand the test of any extensive practical application. His position was, indeed, a very difficult one, the natural allies and supporters of the Papacy being, without exception, the natural enemies of the new ideas to which he had so incautiously opened the door.

Margaret relates various attempts made by Austrians in Lombardy and by Oscurantists in Rome to excite the people to overt acts of violence, and thus gain a pretext for the employment of armed force. In Rome, on New Year's day, an attempt of this sort was near succeeding, the governor of the city having ungraciously forbidden the people to wait upon the Pope at the Quirinal, and to ask for his blessing. For-

tunately, instead of rising in rebellion, they betook themselves to Senator Corsini, by whose
friendly interposition the Pope was induced to
make a progress through the city, interrupted
only by the prayers of his subjects, who, falling
on their knees as he passed, cried out: "Holy
Father, don't desert us! don't forget us! don't
listen to our enemies!" the Pope, in tears, re-
plying: "Fear nothing, my people; my heart
is yours." And this tender-hearted populace,
seeing that the Pope looked ill, and that the
weather was inclement, begged him to return to
the Quirinal, which he did, the popular leader,
Ciceruacchio, following his carriage.

A letter from Mazzini to Pope Pius, printed in
Paris, had reached Italy by this time, and was
translated by Margaret for publication in the
"New York Tribune." Some passages of it
will not be out of place here, as showing the
position and outlook of a man by far the most
illustrious of the Italian exiles, and one whose
purity of life and excellence of character gave
to his opinions a weight beyond their intellectual value.

After introducing himself as one who adores
God, Mazzini says that he adores, also, an idea
which seems to him to be of God, that of Italy
as "an angel of moral unity and of progressive
civilization for the nations of Europe."

15

Having studied the great history of humanity, and having there found " Rome twice directress of the world, first through the Emperors, later through the Popes," he is led to believe that the great city is destined to a third and more lasting period of supremacy.

" I believe that another European world ought to be revealed from the Eternal City, that had the Capitol and has the Vatican. And this faith has not abandoned me through years, poverty, and griefs which God alone knows."

One cannot help pausing here to reflect that in both historic instances the supremacy of Rome was due to a superiority of civilization which she has long lost, and is not likely to regain in this day of the world.

Mazzini says to the Pope: " There is no man this day in all Europe more powerful than you ; you then have, most Holy Father, vast duties."

He now passes on to a review of the situation : —

" Europe is in a tremendous crisis of doubts and desires. Faith is dead. Catholicism is lost in despotism ; Protestantism is lost in anarchy. The intellect travels in a void. The bad adore calculation, physical good ; the good pray and hope ; nobody believes. . . .

" I call upon you, after so many ages of doubt and corruption, to be the apostle of eternal

truth. I call upon you to make yourself the
'servant of all;' to sacrifice yourself, if needful,
so that the will of God may be done on earth as
it is in heaven; to hold yourself ready to glorify
God in victory, or to repeat with resignation, if
you must fail, the words of Gregory VII.: 'I
die in exile because I have loved justice and
hated iniquity.'

"But for this, to fulfil the mission which God
confides to you, two things are needful, — to be
a believer, and to unify Italy."

The first of these two clauses is here amplified
into an exhortation which, edifying in itself, had
in it nothing likely to suggest to the person
addressed any practical solution of the difficulties which surrounded him.

Having shown the Head of Christendom the
way to right belief, Mazzini next instructs him
how to unify Italy: —

"For this you have no need to work, but [only
to] bless Him who works through you and in
your name. Gather round you those who best
represent the national party. Do not beg alli-
ances with princes. Say, 'The unity of Italy
ought to be a fact of the nineteenth century,'
and it will suffice. Leave our pens free; leave
free the circulation of ideas in what regards this
point, vital for us, of the national unity."

Here follow some special directions with re-

gard to the several powers to be dealt with in the
projected unification. The result of all this, foreseen by Mazzini, would be the foundation of "a
government unique in Europe, which shall destroy the absurd divorce between spiritual and
temporal power, and in which you shall be chosen
to represent the principle of which the men
chosen by the nation will make the application."

"The unity of Italy," says Mazzini, "is a work
of God. It will be fulfilled, with you or without
you. But I address you because I believe you
worthy to take the initiative in a work so vast;
. . . because the revival of Italy, under the ægis
of a religious idea of a standard, not of rights,
but of duties, would leave behind all the revo-
lutions of other countries, and place her immediately at the head of European progress."

Pure and devout as are the sentiments uttered
in this letter, the views which accompany them
have been shown, by subsequent events, to be
only partially just, only partially realizable. The
unification of Italy may to-day be called "a work
of God;" but had it been accomplished on the
theocratic basis imagined by Mazzini, it could
not have led either Europe or Italy itself to the
point now reached through manifold endeavor
and experience. Spirits may be summoned from
the upper air as well as from the "vasty deep,"
but they will not come until the time is ripe for

their work. And yet are prayer and prophecy of this sort sacred and indispensable functions in the priesthood of ideas.

On March 29, 1848, Margaret is able to praise once more the beauty of the scene around her : —

"Now the Italian heavens wear again their deep blue. The sun is glorious, the melancholy lustres are stealing again over the Campagna, and hundreds of larks sing unwearied above its ruins. Nature seems in sympathy with the great events that are transpiring."

What were these events, which, Margaret says, stunned her by the rapidity and grandeur of their march?

The face of Italy was changed indeed. Sicily was in revolt, Naples in revolution. Milan, Venice, Modena, and Parma were driving out their tyrants; and in Rome, men and women were weeping and dancing for joy at the news. Abroad, Louis Philippe had lost his throne, and Metternich his power. Margaret saw the Austrian arms dragged through the streets, and burned in the Piazza del Popolo. "The Italians embraced one another, and cried, *Miracolo! Providenza!* The Tribune Ciceruacchio fed the flame with fagots. Adam Mickiewicz, the great poet of Poland, long exiled from his country, looked on." The double-headed Austrian

eagle was torn from the front of the Palazzo di
Venezia, and in his place was set the inscription,
" Alta Italia." By April 1st the Austrian Vice-
roy had capitulated at Verona, and Italy appeared
to be, or was for the time, " free, independent,
and one."

Poor Pope Pius, meanwhile, had fallen more
and more into the rear of the advancing movement, and finally kept step with it only as he was
compelled to do, secretly looking for the moment
when he should be able to break from the ranks
which he himself had once led. On May 7th,
Margaret writes of his " final dereliction to the
cause of freedom," by which phrase she describes
his refusal to declare war against Austria, after
having himself done and approved of much
which led in that direction. The position of
the Pontiff was now most unhappy. Alarmed
at the agitation and turmoil about him, it is
probable that he bitterly regretted the acts in
which he had been sincere, but of which he had
not foreseen the consequences. Margaret describes him as isolated in his palace, guided by
his confessor, weak and treacherous in his movements, privately disowning the measures which
the popular feeling compelled him to allow, and
secretly doing his utmost to counteract them.

In the month of May Margaret enjoyed some
excursions into the environs of Rome. She vis-

ited Albano, Frascati, and Ostia, and passed some days at Subiaco and at Tivoli. On the 28th of the same month she left Rome for the summer, and retired to Aquila, a little ruined town in the Abruzzi Mountains, where, after so many painful excitements, she hoped to find tranquillity and rest.

CHAPTER XIV.

THE story of this summer in the mountains
Margaret never told, and her letters of the previous winter gave no account of matters most
personal to herself. In continuing the narrative
of her life, we are therefore obliged to break
through the reserves of the moment, and to
speak of events which, though occurring at this
time, were not made known to her most intimate
friends until a much later period.

Margaret had been privately married for some
months when she left Rome for Aquila. Her
husband was a young Italian nobleman, Ossoli

by name, whose exterior is thus described by one
of her most valued friends [1] : —

"He appeared to be of a reserved and gentle
nature, with quiet, gentlemanlike manners ; and
there was something melancholy in the expression of his face which made one desire to know
more of him. In figure he was tall, and of slen-
der frame, with dark hair and eyes. We judged
that he was about thirty years of age, possibly
younger."

Margaret had made the acquaintance of this
gentleman during her first visit to Rome, in the
spring of the year 1847, and under the following
circumstances : She had gone with some friends
to attend the vesper service at St. Peter's, and,
wandering from one point of interest to another
in the vast church, had lost sight of her party.
All efforts to rejoin them proved useless, and
Margaret was in some perplexity, when a young
man of gentlemanly address accosted her, and
asked leave to assist her in finding her friends.
These had already left the church, and by the
time that this became evident to Margaret and
her unknown companion, the hour was late, and
the carriages, which can usually be found in
front of the church after service, had all disappeared. Margaret was therefore obliged to walk
from the Vatican to her lodgings on the Corso,

[1] Mrs. Story, wife of the eminent sculptor.

accompanied by her new friend, with whom she was able at the time to exchange very little conversation. Familiar as she was with Italian literature, the sound of the language was new to her, and its use difficult.

The result of this chance meeting seems to have been love at first sight on the part of the Marchese Ossoli. Before Margaret left Rome he had offered her his hand, and had been refused.

Margaret returned to Rome, as we have seen, in the autumn of the same year. Her acquaintance with the Marchese was now renewed, and with the advantage that she had become sufficiently familiar with the Italian language to converse in it with comparative ease. Her intense interest in the affairs of Italy suggested to him also ideas of "liberty and better government." His education, much neglected, as she thought, had been in the traditions of the narrowest conservatism ; but Margaret's influence led or enabled him to free himself from the trammels of old-time prejudice, and to espouse, with his whole heart, the cause of Roman liberty.

According to the best authority extant, the marriage of Margaret and the Marchese took place in the December following her return to Rome. The father of the Marchese had died but a short time before this, and his estate, left

'n the hands of two other sons, was not yet settled. These gentlemen were both attached to
the Papal household, and, we judge, to the reac-
tionary party. The fear lest the Marchese's
marriage with a Protestant should deprive him
wholly, or in part, of his paternal inheritance, induced the newly married couple to keep to themselves the secret of their relation to each other.
At the moment, ecclesiastical influence would
have been very likely, under such circumstances,
to affect the legal action to be taken in the division of the property. Better things were hoped
for in view of a probable change of government.
So the winter passed, and Margaret went to her
retreat among the mountains, with her secret
unguessed and probably unsuspected.

Her husband was a member — perhaps already
a captain — of the Civic Guard, and was detained
in Rome by military duties. Margaret was
therefore much alone in the midst of "a theatre of glorious, snow-crowned mountains, whose
pedestals are garlanded with the olive and mul-
berry, and along whose sides run bridle-paths
fringed with almond groves and vineyards."
The scene was to her one of "intoxicating beauty," but the distance from her husband soon became more than she could bear. After a month
passed in this place, she found a nearer retreat
at Rieti, also a mountain-town, but within the

confines of the Papal States.   Here Ossoli could sometimes pass the Sunday with her, by travelling in the night.   In one of her letters Margaret writes : " Do not fail to come.   I shall have your coffee warm.   You will arrive early, and I can see the diligence pass the bridge from my window."

In the month of August the Civic Guard were ordered to prepare for a march to Bologna ; and Ossoli, writing to Margaret on the 17th, strongly expresses his unwillingness to be so far removed from her at a time in which she might have urgent need of his presence at any moment.   For these were to her days of great hope and expectation. Her confinement was near at hand, and she was alone, poor and friendless, among people whose only aim was to plunder her.   But Margaret could not, even in these trying circumstances, belie the heroic principles which had always guided her life.   She writes to her doubting, almost despairing husband : " If honor requires it, go.   I will try to sustain myself."

This dreaded trial was averted.   The march to Bologna was countermanded.   Margaret's boy saw the light on the 5th of September, and the joyful presence of her husband soothed for her the pangs of a first maternity.

He was indeed obliged to leave her the next day for Rome.   Margaret was ill cared for, and lost, through a severe fever, the ability to nurse her child. She was forced to dismiss her only attendant, and to struggle in her helpless condition with the dishonesty and meanness of the people around her. A *balia*[1] for the child was soon found, but Margaret felt the need of much courage in guarding the first days of her infant's life. In her eyes he grew " more beautiful every hour." The people in the house called him Angiolino, anticipating the name afterwards given him in baptism, — Angelo Eugene.

She was soon to find a new trial in leaving him. Her husband still wished to keep his marriage a profound secret, and to this end desired that the baby should be left at Rieti, in charge of " a good nurse who should treat him like a mother." Margaret was most anxious to return to Rome, to be near her husband, and also in order to be able to carry on the literary labor upon which depended not only her own support, but also that of her child.

Writing to Ossoli, she says : " I cannot stay long without seeing the boy. He is so dear, and life seems so uncertain. It is necessary that I should be in Rome a month at least, to write, and to be near you. But I must be free to return here, if I feel too anxious and suffering for him."

[1] Wet-nurse.

Early in November Margaret returned to
Rome. In a letter to her mother, bearing the
date of November 16, she says : —

"I am again in Rome, situated for the first
time entirely to my mind. . . . I have the sun
all day, and an excellent chimney. It [her lodg-
ing] is very high, and has pure air, and the most
beautiful view all around imaginable. . . . The
house looks out on the Piazza Barberini, and I see
both that palace and the Pope's [the Quirinal]."

The assassination of the Minister Rossi had
taken place on the previous day. Margaret describes it almost as if she had seen it : —

"The poor, weak Pope has fallen more and
more under the dominion of the cardinals. He
had suffered the Minister Rossi to go on, tight-
ening the reins, and because the people preserved a sullen silence, he thought they would
bear it. . . . Rossi, after two or three most un-
popular measures, had the imprudence to call
the troops of the line to defend him, instead of
the National Guard. . . . Yesterday, as he descended from his carriage to enter the Chamber [of Deputies], the crowd howled and hissed,
then pushed him, and as he turned his head in
consequence, a sure hand stabbed him in the
back."

On the morrow, the troops and the people united
in calling upon the Pope, then at the Quirinal,

for a change of measures. They found no audience, but only the hated Swiss mercenaries, who defeated an attempt to enter the palace by firing on the crowd. " The drum beat to call out the National Guard. The carriage of Prince Barberini has returned, with its frightened inmates and liveried retinue, and they have suddenly barred up the court-yard gate." Margaret felt no apprehension for herself in all this turmoil. The side which had, for the moment, the upper hand, was her own, and these very days were such as she had longed for, not, we may be sure, for their accompaniments of bloodshed and violence, but for the outlook which was to her and her friends one of absolute promise.

The " good time coming " did then seem to have come for Italy. Her various populations had risen against their respective tyrants, and had shown a disposition to forget past divisions in the joy of a country reconciled and united.

In the principal churches of Rome, masses were performed in commemoration of the patriotic men who fell at this time in various struggles with existing governments. Thus were honored the "victims" of Milan, of Naples, of Venice, of Vienna.

Not long after the assassination of Rossi, the Pope, imploring the protection of the King of Naples, fled to Gaeta.

" No more of him," writes Margaret; "his day is over. He has been made, it seems unconsciously, an instrument of good which his regrets cannot destroy."

The political consequences of this act were scarcely foreseen by the Romans, who, according to Margaret's account, remained quite cool and composed, saying only: " The Pope, the cardinals, the princes are gone, and Rome is perfectly tranquil. One does not miss anything, except that there are not so many rich carriages and liveries."

In February Margaret chronicles the opening of the Constitutional Assembly, which was heralded by a fine procession, with much display of banners. In this, Prince Canino, a nephew of Napoleon, walked side by side with Garibaldi, both having been chosen deputies. Margaret saw this from a balcony in the Piazza di Venezia, whose stern old palace "seemed to frown, as the bands each, in passing, struck up the *Marseillaise.*" On February 9th the bells were rung in honor of the formation of a Roman Republic. The next day Margaret went forth early, to observe the face of Rome. She saw the procession of deputies mount the Campidoglio (Capitol), with the Guardia Civica for their escort. Here was promulgated the decree announcing the formation of the Republic, and guarantee-

ing to the Pope the undisturbed exercise of his
spiritual power.

The Grand Duke of Tuscany now fled, smiling
assent to liberal principles as he entered his
carriage to depart. The King of Sardinia was
naturally filled with alarm. " It makes no difference," says Margaret. " He and his minister,
Gioberti, must go, unless foreign intervention
should impede the liberal movement. In this
case, the question is, what will France do ?
Will she basely forfeit every pledge and every
duty, to say nothing of her true interest ? "
Alas! France was already sold to the coun-
terfeit greatness of a name, and was pledged
to a course irrational and vulgar beyond any
that she had yet followed. The Roman Republic, born of high hope and courage, had
but few days to live, and those days were full
of woe.

Margaret had so made the life of Rome her
own at this period, that we have found it impossible to describe the one without recounting
something of the other. Her intense interest
in public affairs could not, however, wean her
thoughts from the little babe left at Rieti.
Going thither in December, she passed a week
with her darling, but was forced after this to remain three months in Rome without seeing him.
Here she lay awake whole nights, contriving how

16

she might end this painful separation ; but circumstances were too strong for her, and the object so dearly wished for could not be compassed.

In March she visited him again, and found him in health, "and plump, though small." The baby leaned his head pathetically against her breast, seeming, she thought, to say, " How could you leave me?" He is described as a sensitive and precocious little creature, — affected, Margaret thought, by sympathy with her ; "for," she says, " I worked very hard before his birth [at her book on Italy], with the hope that all my spirit might be incarnated in him."

She returned to Rome about the middle of April. The French were already in Italy. Their " web of falsehood " was drawing closer and closer round the devoted city. Margaret was not able to visit her boy again until the siege, soon begun, ended in the downfall of the Roman Republic.

The government of Rome, at this time, was in the hands of a triumvirate, whose names — Armellini, Mazzini, and Saffi — are appended to the official communications made in answer to the letters of the French Envoy, M. de Lesseps, and of the Commander-in-Chief, General Oudinot. The French side of this correspondence presented but a series of tergiversations, the truth being simply that the opportunity of reinstating the Roman Pontiff in his temporal domain was too valuable to be allowed to pass, by the adventurer who then, under the name of President, already ruled France by military despotism. In the great game of hazard which he played, the prospective adhesion of the Pope's spiritual subjects was the highest card he could hold. The people who had been ignorant enough to elect Louis Napoleon, were easily led to justify his outrageous expedition to Rome.

In Margaret's manifold disappointments, Mazzini always remained her ideal of a patriot, and, as she says, of a prince. To her, he stands alone in Italy, "on a sunny height, far above the stature of other men." He came to her lodgings in Rome, and was in appearance "more divine than ever, after all his new, strange sufferings." He had then just been made a Roman citizen, and would in all probability have been made President, had the Republic continued to exist. He talked long with Margaret, and, she says, was not sanguine as to the outcome of the difficulties of the moment.

The city once invested, military hospitals became a necessity. The Princess Belgiojoso, a Milanese by birth, and in her day a social and political notability, undertook to organize these

establishments, and obtained, by personal solici-
tation, the funds necessary to begin her work.
On the 30th of April, 1849, she wrote the following letter to Margaret : —

"DEAR MISS FULLER, — You are named Su-
perintendent of the Hospital of the *Fate Bene
Fratelli.* Go there at twelve, if the alarm-bell
has not rung before. When you arrive there,
you will receive all the women coming for the
wounded, and give them your directions, so that
you are sure to have a number of them, night
and day.

"May God help us!

"CHRISTINE TRIVULZE, OF BELGIOJOSO."

CHAPTER XV.

MARGARET writes to Mr. Emerson in June:
"Since the 30th of April I go almost daily to
the hospitals, and, though I have suffered, for I
had no idea before how terrible gun-shot wounds
and wound-fever are, yet I have taken great pleasure in being with the men. There is scarcely
one who is not moved by a noble spirit."

"Night and day," writes the friend cited above,[1]
" Margaret was occupied, and, with the Princess,

---

[1] Mrs. Story.

so ordered and disposed the hospitals that their conduct was admirable. Of money they had very little, and they were obliged to give their time and thoughts in its place. I have walked through the wards with Margaret, and have seen how comforting was her presence to the poor suffering men. For each one's peculiar tastes she had a care. To one she carried books ; to another she told the news of the day ; and listened to another's oft-repeated tale of wrongs, as the best sympathy she could give. They raised themselves on their elbows to get the last glimpse of her " as she went her way.

Ossoli, meanwhile, was stationed, with his command, on the walls of the Vatican, — a post of considerable danger. This he refused to leave, even for necessary food and rest. The provisions sent him from time to time were shared with his needy comrades. As these men were brought, wounded and dying, to the hospitals, Margaret looked eagerly to see whether her husband was among them. She was able, sometimes, to visit him at his post, and to talk with him about the beloved child, now completely beyond their reach, as the city was invested on all sides, and no sure means of communication open to them. They remained for many days without any news of the little one, and their first intelligence concerning him was to the effect that the nurse with whom he had been left would at once abandon him unless a certain sum of money should be sent in prepayment of her services. This it seemed at first impossible to do ; but after a while the money was sent, and the evil day adjourned for a time.

Margaret's letters of the 10th of June speak of a terrible battle recently fought between the French troops and the defenders of Rome. The Italians, she says, fought like lions, making a stand for honor and conscience' sake, with scarcely any prospect of success. The attack of the enemy was directed with a skill and order which Margaret was compelled to admire. The loss on both sides was heavy, and the assailants, for the moment, gained " no inch of ground." But this was only the beginning of the dread trial. By the 20th of June the bombardment had become heavy. On the night of the 21st a practicable breach was made, and the French were within the city. The defence, however, was valiantly continued until the 30th, when Garibaldi informed the Assembly that further resistance would be useless. Conditions of surrender were then asked for and refused. Garibaldi himself was denied a safe-conduct, and departed with his troops augmented by a number of soldiers from other regiments. This was on July 2d, after it became known that the

French army would take possession on the morrow. Margaret followed the departing troops
as far as the Place of St. John Lateran. Never
had she seen a sight "so beautiful, so romantic,
and so sad."

The grand piazza had once been the scene of
Rienzi's triumph: "The sun was setting, the
crescent moon rising, the flower of the Italian
youth were marshalling in that solemn place.
They had all put on the beautiful dress of the
Garibaldi legion, — the tunic of bright red cloth,
the Greek cap, or round hat with puritan plume.
Their long hair was blown back from resolute
faces. . . . I saw the wounded, all that could
go, laden upon their baggage-cars. I saw many
youths, born to rich inheritance, carrying in a
handkerchief all their worldly goods. The wife
of Garibaldi followed him on horseback. He
himself was distinguished by the white tunic.
His look was entirely that of a hero of the
Middle Ages, — his face still young. . . . He
went upon the parapet, and looked upon the
road with a spy-glass, and, no obstruction being
in sight, he turned his face for a moment back
upon Rome, then led the way through the gate."

Thus ended the heroic defence of Rome.
The French occupation began on the next day,
with martial law and the end of all liberties.
Alas! that it was not given to Margaret to

see Garibaldi come again, with the laurels of an abiding victory! Alas! that she saw not the end of the Napoleon game, and the punishment of France for her act of insensate folly!

It was during these days of fearful trial and anxiety that Margaret confided to Mrs. Story the secret of her marriage. This was done, not for the relief of her own overtasked feelings, but in the interest of her child, liable at this time to be left friendless by the death of his parents. Margaret, in her extreme anxiety concerning her husband's safety, became so ill and feeble that the duration of her own life appeared to her very uncertain. In a moment of great depression she called Mrs. Story to her bedside, related to her all the antecedents of the birth of the child, and showed her, among other papers, the certificate of her marriage, and of her son's legal right to inherit the title and estate of his father. These papers she intrusted to Mrs. Story's care, requesting her, in case of her own death, to seek her boy at Rieti, and to convey him to her friends in America.

To Lewis Cass, at that time American Envoy to the Papal Court, the same secret was confided, and under circumstances still more trying. Shortly before the conclusion of the siege, Margaret learned that an attack would probably be made upon the very part of the city in which

Ossoli was stationed with his men. She accordingly sent to request that Mr. Cass would call upon her at once, which he did. He found her "lying on a sofa, pale and trembling, evidently much exhausted." After informing him of her marriage, and of the birth and whereabouts of her child, she confided to his care certain important documents, to be sent, in the event of her death, to her family in America. Her husband was, at that very moment, in command of a battery directly exposed to the fire of the French artillery. The night before had been one of great danger to him, and Margaret, in view of his almost certain death, had determined to pass the coming night at his post with him, and to share his fate, whatever it might be. He had promised to come for her at the Ave Maria, and Mr. Cass, departing, met him at the porter's lodge, and shortly afterward beheld them walking in the direction of his command. It turned out that the threatened danger did not visit them. The cannonading from this point was not renewed, and on the morrow military operations were at an end.

Among our few pictures of Margaret and her husband, how characteristic is this one, of the pair walking side by side into the very jaws of death, with the glory of faith and courage bright about them !

The gates once open, Margaret's first thought was of Rieti, and her boy there. Thither she sped without delay, arriving just in time to save the life of the neglected and forsaken child, whose wicked nurse, uncertain of further payment, had indeed abandoned him. His mother found him " worn to a skeleton, too weak to smile, or lift his little wasted hand." Four weeks of incessant care and nursing brought, still in wan feebleness, his first returning smile.

All that Margaret had already endured seemed to her light in comparison with this. In the Papal States, woman had clearly fallen behind even the standard of the she-wolf.

After these painful excitements came a season of blessed quietness for Margaret and her dear ones. Angelo regained his infant graces, and became full of life and of baby glee. Margaret's marriage was suitably acknowledged, and the pain and trouble of such a concealment were at end. The disclosure of the relation naturally excited much comment in Italy and in America. In both countries there were some, no doubt, who chose to interpret this unexpected action on the part of Margaret in a manner utterly at variance with the whole tenor and spirit of her life. The general feeling was, however, quite otherwise ; and it is gratifying to find that, while no one could have considered Margaret's marriage an act of worldly wisdom, it was very generally accepted by her friends as only another instance of the romantic disinterestedness which had always been a leading trait in her character.

Writing to an intimate friend in America, she remarks: "What you say of the meddling curiosity of people repels me; it is so different here. When I made my appearance with a husband, and a child of a year old, nobody did the least act to annoy me. All were most cordial; none asked or implied questions."

She had already written to Madame Arconati, asking whether the fact of her concealed marriage and motherhood would make any difference in their relations. Her friend, a lady of the highest position and character, replied: "What difference can it make, except that I shall love you more, now that we can sympathize as mothers?"

In other letters, Margaret speaks of the loving sympathy expressed for her by relatives in America. The attitude of her brothers was such as she had rightly expected it to be. Her mother received the communication in the highest spirit, feeling assured that a leading motive in Margaret's withholding of confidence from her had been the desire to spare her a season of most painful anxiety. Speaking of a letter recently received from her, Margaret says:—

" She blessed us. She rejoiced that she should not die feeling there was no one left to love me with the devotion she thought I needed. She expressed no regret at our poverty, but offered her feeble means."

After a stay of some weeks at Rieti, Margaret, with her husband and child, journeyed to Perugia, and thence to Florence. At the former place she remained long enough to read D' Azeglio's " Nicolò dei Lapi," which she esteemed "a book unenlivened by a spark of genius, but interesting as illustrative of Florence." Here she felt that she understood, for the first time, the depth and tenderness of the Umbrian school.

The party reached Florence late in September, and were soon established in lodgings for the winter. The police at first made some objection to their remaining in the city, but this matter was soon settled to their satisfaction. Margaret's thoughts now turned toward her own country and her own people : —

" It will be sad to leave Italy, uncertain of return. Yet when I think of you, beloved mother, of brothers and sisters and many friends, I wish to come. Ossoli is perfectly willing. He will go among strangers ; but to him, as to all the young Italians, America seems the land of liberty."

Margaret's home-letters give lovely glimpses

of this season of peace. Her modest establishment was served by Angelo's nurse, with a little occasional aid from the porter's wife. The boy himself was now in rosy health ; as his mother says, " a very gay, impetuous, ardent, but sweet-tempered child." She describes with a mother's delight his visit to her room at first waking, when he pulls her curtain aside, and goes through his pretty routine of baby tricks for her amusement, — laughing, crowing, imitating the sound of the bellows, and even saying " Bravo ! " Then comes his bath, which she herself gives him, and then his walk and mid-day sleep.

" I feel so refreshed by his young life, and Ossoli diffuses such a power and sweetness over every day, that I cannot endure to think yet of our future. We have resolved to enjoy being together as much as we can in this brief interval, perhaps all we shall ever know of peace. I rejoice in all that Ossoli did (in the interest of the liberal party); but the results are disastrous, especially as my strength is now so impaired. This much I hope, in life or death, to be no more separated from Angelo."

Margaret's future did indeed look to her full of difficult duties. At forty years of age, having labored all her life for her father's family, she was to begin a new struggle for her own. She had looked this necessity bravely in the face, and

with resolute hand had worked at a history of
recent events in Italy, hoping thus to make a
start in the second act of her life-work. The
two volumes which she had completed by this
time seemed to her impaired in value by the
intense, personal suffering which had lain like
a weight upon her. Such leisure as the care of
Angelo left her, while in Florence, was employed
in the continuation of this work, whose loss we
deplore the more for the intense personal feeling
which must have throbbed through its pages.
Margaret had hoped to pass this winter without
any enforced literary labor, learning of her child,
as she wisely says, and as no doubt she did,
whatever else she may have found it necessary
to do. In the chronicle of her days he plays
an important part, his baby laugh "all dimples
and glitter," his contentment in the fair scene
about him when, carried to the *Cascine*, he lies
back in her arms, smiling, singing to himself,
and moving his tiny feet. The Christmas holi-
days are dearer to her than ever before, for his
sake. In the evening, before the bright little
fire, he sits on his stool between father and
mother, reminding Margaret of the days in
which she had been so seated between her own
parents. He is to her "a source of ineffable
joys, far purer, deeper, than anything I ever
felt before."

As Margaret's husband was destined to remain a tradition only to the greater number of her friends, the hints and outlines of him given here and there in her letters are important, in showing us what companionship she had gained in return for her great sacrifice.

Ossoli seems to have belonged to a type of character the very opposite of that which Margaret had best known and most admired. To one wearied with the over-intellection and restless aspiration of the accomplished New Englander of that time, the simple geniality of the Italian nature had all the charm of novelty and contrast. Margaret had delighted in the race from her first acquaintance with it, but had found its happy endowments heavily weighted with traits of meanness and ferocity. In her husband she found its most worthy features, and her heart, wearied with long seeking and wandering, rested at last in the confidence of a simple and faithful attachment.

She writes from Florence: " My love for Ossoli is most pure and tender ; nor has any one, except my mother or little children, loved me so genuinely as he does. To some, I have been obliged to make myself known. Others have loved me with a mixture of fancy and enthusiasm, excited at my talent of embellishing life. But Ossoli loves me from simple affinity ;

he loves to be with me, and to serve and soothe
me."

And in another letter she says : " Ossoli will
be a good father. He has very little of what is
called intellectual development, but has unspoiled
instincts, affections pure and constant, and a quiet
sense of duty which, to me who have seen much
of the great faults in characters of enthusiasm
and genius, seems of highest value."

Some reminiscences contributed by the accomplished *littérateur*, William Henry Hurlbut,
will help to complete the dim portrait of the
Marchese : —

" The frank and simple recognition of his
wife's singular nobleness, which he always dis-
played, was the best evidence that his own nature was of a fine and noble strain. And those
who knew him best are, I believe, unanimous in
testifying that his character did in no respect
belie the evidence borne by his manly and truth-
ful countenance to its warmth and sincerity.
He seemed quite absorbed in his wife and child.
I cannot remember ever to have found Madame
Ossoli alone, on the evenings when she remained
at home."

Mr. Hurlbut says further: " Notwithstanding
his general reserve and curtness of speech, on
two or three occasions he showed himself to
possess quite a quick and vivid fancy, and even a

17

certain share of humor. I have heard him tell stories remarkably well. One tale especially, which related to a dream he had in early life, I remember as being told with great felicity and vivacity of expression."

Though opposed, like all liberals, to the ecclesiastical government of Rome, the Marchese appeared to Mr. Hurlbut a devout Catholic. He often attended vesper services in Florence, and Margaret, unwavering in her Protestantism, still found it sweet to kneel by his side.

Margaret read, this winter, Louis Blanc's "Story of Ten Years," and Lamartine's "Girondists." Her days were divided between family cares and her literary work, which for the time consisted in recording her impressions of recent events. She sometimes passed an evening at the rooms occupied by the Mozier and Chapman families, where the Americans then resident in Florence were often gathered together. She met Mr. and Mrs. Browning often, and with great pleasure. The Marchesa Arconati she saw almost daily.

One of Margaret's last descriptions is of the Duomo,[1] which she visited with her husband on Christmas eve : —

"No one was there. Only the altars were lit up, and the priests, who were singing, could not

---

[1] Cathedral.

be seen by the faint light. The vast solemnity of the interior is thus really felt. The Duomo is more divine than St. Peter's, and worthy of genius pure and unbroken. St. Peter's is, like Rome, a mixture of sublimest heaven with corruptest earth. I adore the Duomo, though no place can now be to me like St. Peter's, where has been passed the splendidest part of my life."

Thus looked to her, in remembrance, the spot where she had first met her husband, where she had shared his heroic vigils, and stood beside him within reach of death.

The little household suffered some inconvenience before the winter was over. By the middle of December the weather became severely cold, and Margaret once more experienced the inconvenience of ordinary lodgings in Italy, in which the means of heating the rooms are very limited. The baby grew impatient of confinement, and constantly pointed to the door, which he was not allowed to pass. Of their several rooms, one only was comfortable under these circumstances. Of this, as occupied in the winter evenings, Mr. Hurlbut has given a pleasant description : --

" A small, square room, sparingly yet sufficiently furnished, with polished floor and frescoed ceiling ; and, drawn up closely before the cheerful fire, an oval table, on which stood a monkish lamp of brass, with depending chains that support quaint classic cups for the olive oil. There, seated beside his wife, I was sure to find the Marchese, reading from some patriotic book, and dressed in the dark brown, red-corded coat of the Guardia Civica, which it was his melancholy pleasure to wear at home. So long as the conversation could be carried on in Italian, he used to remain, though he rarely joined in it to any considerable degree. If many *forestieri* [1] chanced to drop in, he betook himself to a neighboring *café*, — not absenting himself through aversion to such visitors, but in the fear lest his silent presence might weigh upon them."

To complete the picture here given of the Ossoli interior, we should mention Horace, the youngest brother of Charles Sumner, who was a daily visitor in this abode of peace. Margaret says of him : " He has solid good in his mind and heart. . . When I am ill, or in a hurry, he helps me like a brother. Ossoli and Sumner exchange some instruction in English and Italian."

This young man, remembered by those who knew him as most amiable and estimable, was abroad at this time for his health, and passed

[1] Foreigners.

the winter in Florence. Mr. Hurlbut tells us that he brought Margaret, every morning, his tribute of fresh wild flowers, and that every evening, "beside her seat in her little room, his mild, pure face was to be seen, bright with a quiet happiness," which was in part derived from her kindness and sympathy.

This brief chronicle of Margaret's last days in Italy would be incomplete without a few words concerning the enviable position which she had made for herself in this country of her adoption.

The way in which the intelligence of her marriage was received by her country-people in Rome and Florence gives the strongest proof of the great esteem in which they were constrained to hold her. Equally honorable to her was the friendship of Madame Arconati, a lady of high rank and higher merit, beloved and revered as few were in the Milan of that day. She was the friend of Joseph Mazzini, and shared with George Sand and Elizabeth Barrett Browning the honors of prominence in the liberal movement and aspiration of the time. But it is in her intercourse with the people at large that we shall find the deepest evidence of her true humanity. Hers was no barren creed, divorced from beneficent action. The wounded soldiers in the hospital, the rude peasants of

Rieti, knew her heart, and thought of her as "a mild saint and ministering angel." [1] Ferocious and grasping as these peasants were, she was able to overcome for the time their savage instincts, and to turn the tide of their ungoverned passions.

In this place, two brothers were one day saved from the guilt of fratricide by her calm and firm intervention. Both of the men were furiously angry, and blood had already been drawn by the knife of one, when she stepped between them, and so reasoned and insisted, that the weapons were presently flung away, and the feud healed by a fraternal embrace. After this occurrence, the American lady was recognized as a peacemaker, and differences of various sorts were referred to her for settlement, much as domestic and personal difficulties had been submitted to her in her own New England.

Among the troubles brought under her notice at Rieti were the constant annoyances caused by the lawless behavior of a number of Spanish troops who happened to be quartered upon the town. Between these and the villagers she succeeded in keeping the peace by means of good counsel and enforced patience. In Florence she seems to have been equally beloved and respected. A quarrel here took place between

[1] Mrs. Story's reminiscences.

her maid, from Rieti, and a fellow-lodger, in which her earnest effort prevented bloodshed, and effectually healed the breach between the two women. The porter of the house in which she dwelt while in Florence was slowly dying of consumption ; Margaret's kindness so attached him to her that he always spoke of her as *la cara signora.*

The unruly Garibaldi Legion overtook Margaret one day between Rome and Rieti. She had been to visit her child at the latter place, and was returning to Rome alone in a vettura. While she was resting for an hour at a wayside inn, the master of the house entered in great alarm, crying : " We are lost ! Here is the Legion Garibaldi ! These men always pillage, and, if we do not give all up to them without pay, they will kill us." Looking out upon the road, Margaret saw that the men so much dreaded were indeed close at hand. For a moment she felt some alarm, thinking that they might insist upon taking the horses from her carriage, and thus render it impossible for her to proceed on her journey. Another moment, and she had found a device to touch their better nature. As the troop entered, noisy and disorderly, Margaret rose and said to the innkeeper : " Give these good men bread and wine at my expense, for after their ride they must need refreshment." The men at once became quiet and respectful. They partook of the offered hospitality with the best grace, and at parting escorted her to her carriage, and took leave of her with great deference. She drove off, wondering at their bad reputation. They probably were equally astonished at her dignity and friendliness.

The statements of Margaret's friends touch us with their account of the charities which this poor woman was able to afford through economy and self-sacrifice. When she allowed herself only the bare necessaries of living and diet, she could have the courage to lend fifty dollars to an artist whom she deemed poorer than herself. Rich indeed was this generous heart, to an e. tent undreamed of by wealthy collectors and pleasure-seekers.

CHAPTER XVI.

RETURN to her own country now lay immediately before Margaret. In the land of her adoption the struggle for freedom had failed, and no
human foresight could have predicted the period
of its renewal. Europe had cried out, like the
sluggard on his bed : "You have waked me too
soon ; I must slumber again."

Margaret's delight in the new beauties and
resources unfolded to her in various European
countries, and especially in Italy, had made the
thought of this return unwelcome to her. But
now that free thought had become contraband
in the beautiful land, where should she carry her
high-hearted hopes, if not westward, with the
tide of the true empire that shall grow out of
man's conquest of his own brute passions ?

This holy westward way, found of Columbus,
broadened and brightened by the Pilgrims, and

become an ocean highway for the nations of the earth, lay open to her. From its farther end came to her the loving voices of kindred, and friends of youth. There she, a mother, could "show her babe, and make her boast," to a mother of her own. There brothers, trained to noble manhood through her care and labor, could rise up to requite something of what they owed her. There she could tell the story of her Italy, with the chance of a good hearing. There, where she had sown most precious seed in the field of the younger generations, she would find some sheaves to bind for her own heart-harvest.

And so the last days in Florence came. The vessel was chosen, and the day of sailing fixed upon. Margaret's last letter, addressed to her mother, is dated on the 14th of May.

We read it now with a weight of sorrow which was hidden from her. In the light of what afterwards took place, it has the sweet solemnity of a greeting sent from the borders of another world.

"FLORENCE, May 14, 1850.

"I will believe I shall be welcome with my treasures, — my husband and child. For me, I long so much to see you! Should anything hinder our meeting upon earth, think of your daughter as one who always wished, at least, to do her duty, and who always cherished you, according as her mind opened to discover excellence.

" Give dear love, too, to my brothers ; and first, to my eldest, faithful friend, Eugene ; a sister's love to Ellen ; love to my kind and good aunts, and to my dear cousin E——. God bless them !

" I hope we shall be able to pass some time together yet, in this world. But, if God decrees otherwise, here and hereafter, my dearest mother,
"Your loving child,
"Margaret."

Who is there that reads twice a sorrowful story without entertaining an unreasonable hope that its ending may change in the reperusal ? So does one return to the fate of " Paul and Virginia," so to that of the " Bride of Lammermoor." So, even in the wild tragedy of " Othello," seen for the hundredth time, one still sees a way of escape for the victim ; still, in imagination, implores her to follow it. And when repeated representation has made assurance doubly sure, we yield to the mandate which none can resist, once issued, and say, " It was to be."

This unreasonable struggle renews itself within us as we follow the narrative of Margaret's departure for her native land. Why did she choose a merchant vessel from Leghorn ? why one which was destined to carry in its hold

the heavy marble of Powers's Greek Slave ?
She was warned against this, was uncertain
in her own mind, and disturbed by presages of
ill. But economy was very necessary to her at
the moment. The vessel chosen, the barque
" Elizabeth," was new, strong, and ably commanded. Margaret had seen and made friends
with the captain, Hasty by name, and his wife.
Horace Sumner was to be their fellow-passenger,
and a young Italian girl, Celeste Paolini, engaged
to help in the care of the little boy. These considerations carried the day.

Just before leaving Florence, Margaret received letters the tenor of which would have
enabled her to remain longer in Italy. Ossoli
remembered the warning of a fortune-teller,
who in his childhood had told him to beware of
the sea. Margaret wrote of omens which gave
her " a dark feeling." She had "a vague expectation of some crisis," she knows not what ;
and this year, 1850, had long appeared to her a
period of pause in the ascent of life, a point at
which she should stand, as " on a plateau, and
take more clear and commanding views than ever
before." She prays fervently that she may not
lose her boy at sea, " either by unsolaced illness,
or amid the howling waves ; or if so, that Ossoli,
Angelo, and I may go together, and that the
anguish may be brief."

These presentiments, strangely prophetic, returned upon Margaret with so much force that on the very day appointed for sailing, the 17th of May, she stood at bay before them for an hour, unable to decide whether she should go or stay. But she had appointed a general meeting with her family in July, and had positively engaged her passage in the barque. Fidelity to these engagements prevailed with her. She may have felt, too, the danger of being governed by vague forebodings which, shunning death in one form, often invite it in another. And so, in spite of fears and omens, too well justified in the sequel, she went on board, and the voyage began in smooth tranquillity.

The first days at sea passed quietly enough. The boy played on the deck, or was carried about by the captain. Margaret and her husband suffered little inconvenience from seasickness, and were soon walking together in the limited space of their floating home. But presently the good captain fell ill with small-pox of a malignant type. On June 3d the barque anchored off Gibraltar, the commander breathed his last, and was accorded a seaman's burial, in the sea. Here the ship suffered a detention of some days from unfavorable winds, but on the 9th was able to proceed on her way; and two days later Angelo showed symptoms of the dreadful disease, which visited him severely. His eyes were closed, his head swollen, his body disfigured by the accompanying eruption. Margaret and Ossoli, strangers to the disease, hung over their darling, and nursed him so tenderly that he was in due time restored, not only to health, but also to his baby beauty, so much prized by his mother.

Margaret wrote from Gibraltar, describing the captain's illness and death, and giving a graphic picture of his ocean funeral. She did not at the time foresee Angelo's illness, but knew that he might easily have taken the infection. Relieved from this painful anxiety, the routine of the voyage re-established itself. Ossoli and Sumner continued to instruct each other in their respective languages. The baby became the pet and delight of the sailors. Margaret was busy with her book on Italy, but found time to soothe and comfort the disconsolate widow of the captain after her own availing fashion. Thus passed the summer days at sea. On Thursday, July 18th, the " Elizabeth " was off the Jersey coast, in thick weather, the wind blowing east of south. The former mate was now the captain. Wishing to avoid the coast, he sailed east-north-east, thinking presently to take a pilot, and pass Sandy Hook by favor of the wind.

At night he promised his passengers an early

arrival in New York. They retired to rest in good spirits, having previously made all the usual preparations for going on shore.

By nine o'clock that evening the breeze had become a gale, by midnight a dangerous storm. The commander, casting the lead from time to time, was without apprehension, having, it is supposed, mistaken his locality, and miscalculated the speed of the vessel, which, under close-reefed sails, was nearing the sand-bars of Long Island. Here, on Fire Island beach, she struck, at four o'clock on the morning of July 19th. The main and mizzen masts were promptly cut away, but the heavy marble had broken through the hold, and the waters rushed in. The bow of the vessel stuck fast in the sand, her stern swung around, and she lay with her broadside exposed to the breakers, which swept over her with each returning rise, — a wreck to be saved by no human power.

The passengers sprang from their berths, aroused by the dreadful shock, and guessing but too well its import. Then came the crash of the falling masts, the roar of the waves, as they shattered the cabin skylight and poured down into the cabin, extinguishing the lights. These features of the moment are related as recalled by Mrs. Hasty, sole survivor of the passengers. One scream only was heard from Margaret's state-

room.   Mrs. Hasty and Horace Sumner met in
the cabin and clasped hands.   " We must die ! "
was his exclamation.   " Let us die calmly," said
the resolute woman.   " I hope so," answered he.
The leeward side of the cabin was already under
water, but its windward side still gave shelter,
and here, for three hours, the passengers took
refuge, their feet braced against the long table.
The baby shrieked, as well he might, with the
sudden fright, the noise and chill of the water.
But his mother wrapped him as warmly as she
could, and in her agony cradled him on her
bosom and sang him to sleep.   The girl Celeste
was beside herself with terror ; and here we find
recorded a touching trait of Ossoli, who soothed
her with encouraging words, and touched all
hearts with his fervent prayer.   In the calm of
resignation they now sat conversing with each
other, devising last messages to friends, to be
given by any one of them who might survive
the wreck.

The crew had retired to the top-gallant forecastle, and the passengers, hearing nothing of
them, supposed them to have left the ship.   By
seven o'clock it became evident that the cabin
could not hold together much longer, and Mrs.
Hasty, looking from the door for some way of
escape, saw a figure standing by the foremast,
the space between being constantly swept by the

waves. She tried in vain to make herself heard ; but the mate, Davis, coming to the door of the forecastle, saw her, and immediately ordered the men to go to her assistance. So great was the danger of doing this, that only two of the crew were willing to accompany him. The only refuge for the passengers was now in the forecastle, which, from its position and strength of construction, would be likely to resist longest the violence of the waves. By great effort and coolness the mate and his two companions reached the cabin, and rescued all in it from the destruction so nearly impending. Mrs. Hasty was the first to make the perilous attempt. She was washed into the hatchway, and besought the brave Davis to leave her to her fate ; but he, otherwise minded, caught her long hair between his teeth, and, with true seaman's craft, saved her and himself. Angelo was carried across in a canvas bag hung to the neck of a sailor. Reaching the forecastle, they found a dry and sheltered spot, and wrapped themselves in the sailors' loose jackets, for a little warmth and comfort. The mate three times revisited the cabin, to bring thence various valuables for Mrs. Hasty and Margaret ; and, last of all, a bottle of wine and some figs, that these weary ones might break their fast. Margaret now spoke to Mrs. Hasty of something still left behind, more valuable than money. She would not, however, ask the mate to expose his life again. It is supposed that her words had reference to the manuscript of her work on Italy. From their new position, through the spray and rain they could see the shore, some hundreds of yards off. Men were seen on the beach, but there was nothing to indicate that an attempt would be made to save them. At nine o'clock it was thought that some one of the crew might possibly reach the shore by swimming, and, once there, make some effort to send them aid. Two of the sailors succeeded in doing this. Horace Sumner sprang after them, but sank, unable to struggle with the waves. A last device was that of a plank, with handles of rope attached, upon which the passengers in turn might seat themselves, while a sailor, swimming behind, should guide their course. Mrs. Hasty, young and resolute, led the way in this experiment, the stout mate helping her, and landing her out of the very jaws of death.

And here we fall back into that bootless wishing of which we spoke a little while ago. Oh that Margaret had been willing that the same means should be employed to bring her and hers to land! Again and again, to the very last moment, she was urged to try this way of escape, uncertain, but the only one. It was all in vain.

Margaret would not be separated from her dear ones. Doubtless she continued for a time to hope that some assistance would reach them from the shore. The life-boat was even brought to the beach; but no one was willing to man her, and the delusive hope aroused by her appearance was soon extinguished.

The day wore on; the tide turned. The wreck would not outlast its return. The commanding officer made one last appeal to Margaret before leaving his post. To stay, he told her, was certain and speedy death, as the ship must soon break up. He promised to take her child with him, and to give Celeste, Ossoli, and herself each the aid of an able seaman. Margaret still refused to be parted from child or husband. The crew were then told to "save themselves," and all but four jumped overboard. The commander and several of the seamen reached the shore in safety, though not without wounds and bruises.

By three o'clock in the afternoon the breaking-up was well in progress. Cabin and stern disappeared beneath the waves, and the forecastle filled with water. The little group now took refuge on the deck, and stood about the foremast. Three able-bodied seamen remained with them, and one old sailor, homeward bound for good and all. The deck now parted from the hull, and rose and fell with the sweep of the waves. The final crash must come in a few minutes. The steward now took Angelo in his arms, promising to save him or die. At this very moment the foremast fell, and with it disappeared the deck and those who stood on it. The steward and the child were washed ashore soon after, dead, though not yet cold. The two Italians, Celeste and Ossoli, held for a moment by the rigging, but were swept off by the next wave. Margaret, last seen at the foot of the mast, in her white nightdress, with her long hair hanging about her shoulders, is thought to have sunk at once. Two others, cook and carpenter, were able to save themselves by swimming, and might, alas! have saved her, had she been minded to make the attempt.

What strain of the heroic in her mind overcame the natural instinct to do and dare all upon the chance of saving her own life, and those so dear to her, we shall never know. No doubt the separation involved in any such attempt appeared to her an abandonment of her husband and child. Resting in this idea, she could more easily nerve herself to perish with them than to part from them. She and the babe were feeble creatures to be thrown upon the mercy of the waves, even with the promised aid. Her husband, young and strong, was faithful unto death, and would not leave her. Both

of them, with fervent belief, regarded death as
the entrance to another life, and surely, upon its
very threshold, sought to do their best. So we
must end our questioning and mourning concerning them with a silent acquiescence in what
was to be.

A friend of Margaret, who visited the scene
on the day after the catastrophe, was persuaded
that seven resolute men could have saved every
soul on board the vessel. Through the absence
of proper system and discipline, the life-boat,
though applied for early on the morning of the
wreck, did not arrive until one o'clock in the
afternoon, when the sea had become so swollen
by the storm that it was impossible to launch it.
One hopes, but scarcely believes, that this state
of things has been amended before this time.

The bodies of Margaret and her husband were
never found. That of Angelo was buried at
Fire Island, with much mourning on the part
of the surviving sailors, whose pet and play-
mate he had been. It was afterwards removed
to the cemetery at Mt. Auburn, where, beneath
a marble monument which commemorates the
life and death of his parents, and his own, he
alone lies buried, the only one of Margaret's
treasures that ever reached the country of her
birth.

Death gives an unexpected completeness to the view of individual character. The secret of a noble life is only fully unfolded when its outward envelope has met the fate of all things perishable. And so the mournful tragedy just recounted set its seal upon a career whose endeavor and achievement the world is bound to hold dear. When all that could be known of Margaret was known, it became evident that there was nothing of her which was not heroic in intention; nothing which, truly interpreted, could turn attention from a brilliant exterior to meaner traits allowed and concealed. That she had faults we need not deny; nor that, like other human beings, she needs must have said and done at times what she might afterwards have wished to have better said, better done. But as an example of one who, gifted with great powers, aspired only to their noblest use; who, able to rule, sought rather to counsel and to help, — she deserves a place in the highest niche of her country's affection. As a woman who believed in women, her word is still an evangel of hope and inspiration to her sex. Her heart belonged to all of God's creatures, and most to what is noblest in them. Gray-headed men of to-day, the happy companions of her youth, grow young again while they speak of her. One of these,[1] who is also one of her earlier biographers,

---

[1] James Freeman Clarke.

still recalls her as the greatest soul he ever knew. Such a word, spoken with the weight of ripe wisdom and long experience, may fitly indicate to posterity the honor and reverence which belong to the memory of MARGARET FULLER.

CHAPTER XVII.

THE preceding narrative has necessarily involved some consideration of the writings which gave its subject her place among the authors of her time. This consideration has been carefully interwoven with the story of the life which it was intended to illustrate, not to interrupt. With all this care, however, much has been left unsaid which should be said concerning the value of Margaret's contributions to the critical literature of her time. Of this, our present limits will allow us to make brief mention only.

Margaret so lived in the life of her own day and generation, so keenly felt its good and ill, that many remember her as a woman whose spoken word and presence had in them a power which is but faintly imaged in her writings. Nor is this impression wholly a mistaken one. Certain it is that those who recall the enchantment of her conversation always maintain that the same charm is not to be found in the productions of her pen. Yet if we attentively read what she has left us, without this disparagement, we shall find that it entitles her to a position of honor among the prose writers of her time.

The defects of her style are easily seen. They are in some degree the result of her assiduous study of foreign languages, in which the pure and severe idioms of the English tongue were sometimes lost sight of. Among them may be mentioned a want of measure in expression, and also something akin to the fault which is called on the stage " anti-climax," by which some saying of weight and significance loses its point by being followed by another of equal emphasis. With all this, the high quality of her mind has left its stamp upon all that she gave to the reading public. Much of this first appeared in the form of contributions to the " Tribune," the "Dial," and other journals and magazines. Some of these papers are brief and even fragmentary ; but the shortest of them show careful study and conscientious judgment. All of them are valuable for the admirable view which they present of the time in which Margaret wrote, of its difficulties and limitations, and of the hopes and convictions which, cherished then in the hearts of the few, were destined to make themselves a law to the conscience of the whole community.

The most important of the more elaborate essays is undoubtedly that entitled " Woman in

the Nineteenth Century," of which some account
has already been given in the preceding pages.
Of the four volumes published in 1875, one bears
this title. A second, entitled "Art, Literature,
and the Drama," contains many of the papers
to which reference has been made in our brief
account of Margaret and her contemporaries.
From a third volume, entitled "Abroad and at
Home," we have quoted some of her most interesting statements concerning the liberal movement in Europe, of which she was so ardent a
friend and promoter. A last volume was collected
and published in 1859, by her brother, the Rev.
Arthur B. Fuller, who served as an army chaplain
in the War of the Southern Rebellion, and met
his death on one of its battle-fields. This volume is called "Life Without and Life Within,"
and is spoken of in Mr. Fuller's preface as con-
taining, for the most part, matter never before
given to the world in book form, and also poems
and prose fragments never before published.

In this volume, two papers seem to us to ask
for especial mention. One of these is a review
of Carlyle's "Cromwell," written when the book
was fresh before the public. It deserves to be
read for its felicity of diction, as well as for the
justice of the thought expressed. If we take
into consideration the immense popularity of
Mr. Carlyle in America at the time when this

work of his appeared, we shall prize the courage
and firmness with which Margaret applies to it
her keen power of criticism. The moral insufficiency of the doctrine of the divine right of
force is clearly shown by her; and her own view
of Cromwell's character maintains itself in spite
of the vituperations with which Carlyle visits
those who will not judge his hero as he does.
She even returns these threats with the following humorous passage at arms : —

"Nobody ever doubted his [Cromwell's] great
abilities and force of will; neither doubt we that
he was made an instrument, just as he propo-
seth. But as to looking on him through Mr.
Carlyle's glasses, we shall not be sneered or
stormed into it, unless he has other proof to offer
than is shown yet. . . . If he has become interested in Oliver, or any other pet hyena, by studying his habits, is that any reason why we should
admit him to our pantheon? No! our imbecility
shall keep fast the door against anything short
of proofs that in the hyena a god is incarnated.
. . . We know you do with all your soul love
kings and heroes, Mr. Carlyle, but we are not
sure you would always know the Sauls from the
Davids. We fear, if you had the disposal of
the holy oil, you would be tempted to pour it
on the head of him who is taller by a head than
all his brethren."

Of Cromwell himself, the following is Margaret's estimate :—

"We see a man of strong and wise mind, educated by the pressure of great occasions to the station of command.   We see him wearing the religious garb which was the custom of the times, and even preaching to himself as well as others. But we never see Heaven answering his invocations in any way that can interfere with the rise of his fortunes or the accomplishment of his plans.   To ourselves, the tone of these religious holdings-forth is sufficiently expressive : they all ring hollow. . . . Again, we see Cromwell ruling with a strong arm, and carrying the spirit of monarchy to an excess which no Stuart could surpass. Cromwell, indeed, is wise, and the king he punished with death is foolish : Charles is faithless and Cromwell crafty ; we see no other difference. Cromwell does not in power abide by the principles that led him to it; and we cannot help, so rose-water imbecile are we, admiring those who do.   To us it looks black for one who kills kings to grow to be more kingly than a king."

The other paper of which we desire to speak in this connection, is one treating of the French novelists prominent at the time, and in particular of Balzac, Eugène Sue, and De Vigny.   Of these three names, the first alone retains the prestige which it had when Margaret wrote her

essay. De Vigny, remarkable mostly for purity
of sentiment, finish of style, and a power of setting and limiting his pictures, is a *boudoir* author,
and one read only in boudoirs of studious refinement. Sue, to whose motives Margaret gives
the most humanitarian interpretation, has failed
to commend his method to posterity. His au-
topsy of a diseased state of society is thought to
spread too widely the infection of the evils which
he deplores. His intention is also too humane for
the present day. The world of the last decade
and of the present is too deeply wedded to the
hard worship of money to be touched by the
pathos of women who perish, or of men who
starve. The grievances of the poor against the
rich find to-day no one to give ear to them, and
few even to utter them ; since those who escape
starvation are too busy with beggary and plunder to waste time in such useless musings. Of
the three here cited, Balzac alone remains a king
among novelists ; and Margaret's study of him
imports as much to us to-day as it did to the
world of her time.

She begins by commenting upon the lamentation general at that time, and not uncommon in
this, over the depravity of taste and of life already becoming familiar to the youth of America
through the medium of the French novel. Concerning this, she says : —

" It is useless to bewail what is the inevitable result of the movement of our time. Europe must pour her corruptions no less than her riches on our shores, both in the form of books and of living men. She cannot, if she would, check the tide which bears them hitherward. No defences are possible, on our vast extent of shore, that can preclude their ingress. Our only hope lies in rousing in our own community a soul of goodness, a wise aspiration, that shall give us strength to assimilate this unwholesome food to better substance, or to cast off its contaminations."

In view of the translation and republication of these works, Margaret remarks that it would be desirable for our people to know something of the position which the writers occupy in their own country. She says, moreover, what we would fain hope may be true to-day, that " our imitation of Europe does not yet go so far that the American milliner can be depended on to copy anything from the Parisian grisette, except her cap."

Margaret speaks at some length of Balzac's novel " Le Père Goriot," which she had just read. " The author," she says, " reminds one of the Spanish romancers in the fearlessness with which he takes mud into his hands, and dips his foot in slime. We cannot endure this when done, as by most Frenchmen, with an air of recklessness and gayety ; but Balzac does it with the stern manliness of a Spaniard."

The conception of this novel appears to her " so sublime," that she compares its perusal to a walk through the catacombs, which the reader would not willingly have missed ; " though the light of day seems stained afterwards with the mould of horror and dismay."

She infers from much of its tenor that Balzac was " familiar with that which makes the agony of poverty — its vulgarity.   Dirt, confusion, shabby expedients, living to live, — these are what make poverty terrible and odious ; and in these Balzac would seem to have been steeped to the very lips."   The skill with which he illustrates both the connection and the contrast between the depth of poverty and the height of luxury co-existing in Parisian life, is much dwelt upon by Margaret, as well as the praise-worthy fact that he depicts with equal faithfulness the vices developed by these opposite conditions.   His insight and mastery appear to her " admirable throughout," the characters " excellently drawn," especially that of the Père Goriot, the father of two heartless women, for whom he has sacrificed everything, and who in turn sacrifice him without mercy to their own pleasures and ambitions. Admirable, too, she finds him " in his description of look, tone, gesture. He has a keen sense of whatever is peculiar to the individual." With this acute appreciation of the great novelist's merits, Margaret unites an equally comprehensive perception of his fatal defects of character. His scepticism regarding virtue she calls fearful, his spirit Mephistophelian. "He delights to analyze, to classify. But he has no hatred for what is loathsome, no contempt for what is base, no love for what is lovely, no faith for what is noble. To him there is no virtue and no vice; men and women are more or less finely organized; noble and tender conduct is more agreeable than the reverse, — that is all." His novels show "goodness, aspiration, the loveliest instincts, stifled, strangled by fate in the form of our own brute nature."

Margaret did not, perhaps, foresee how popular strangling of this kind was destined to become in the romance of the period following her own.

Contrasting Eugène Sue with Balzac, she finds in the first an equal power of observation, disturbed by a more variable temperament, and enhanced by "the heart and faith that Balzac lacks." She sees him standing, pen in hand, armed with this slight but keen weapon, as "the champion of poverty, innocence, and humanity against superstition, selfishness, and prejudice." His works, she thinks, with "all their strong points and brilliant decorations, may erelong be forgotten. Still, the writer's .name shall be held in imperishable honor as the teacher of the ignorant, the guardian of the weak." She sums up thus the merits of the two : "Balzac is the heartless surgeon, probing the wounds and describing the delirium of suffering men for the amusement of his students. Sue, a bold and glittering crusader, with endless ballads jingling in the silence of night before the battle." She finds both of them "much right and a good deal wrong," since their most virtuous personages are allowed to practise stratagems, falsehood, and violence, — a taint, she thinks, of the old *régime* under which "La belle France has worn rouge so long that the purest mountain air will not soon restore the natural hues to her complexion."

Two ideal sketches, "The Rich Man" and "The Poor Man," are also preserved in this volume, and are noticeable as treating of differences and difficulties which have rather become aggravated than diminished since Margaret's time. The "Rich Man" is a merchant, who "sees in commerce a representation of most important interests, a grand school that may teach the heart and soul of the civilized world to a willing, thinking mind. He plays his part in the game, but not for himself alone. He sees the interests of

19

all mankind engaged with his, and remembers them while he furthers his own." In regard of his social status, she says : —

"Our nation is not silly in striving for an aristocracy. Humanity longs for its upper classes. The silliness consists in making them out of clothes, equipage, and a servile imitation of foreign manners, instead of the genuine elegance and distinction that can only be produced by genuine culture. . . . Our merchant shall be a real nobleman, whose noble manners spring from a noble mind ; his fashions from a sincere, intelligent love of the beautiful."

"Margaret's 'Poor Man' is an industrious artisan, not too poor to be sure of daily bread, cleanliness, and reasonable comfort. His advantages will be in the harder training and deeper experience which his circumstances will involve. Suffering privation in his own person, he will, she thinks, feel for the sufferings of others. Having no adventitious aids to bring him into prominence, there will be small chance for him "to escape a well-tempered modesty." He must learn enough to convince himself that mental growth and refinement are not secured by one set of employments, or lost through another. "Mahomet was not a wealthy merchant ; profound philosophers have ripened on the benches, not of the lawyers, but of the shoemakers. It did not hurt Milton to be a school-master, nor Shakespeare to do the errands of a London playhouse. Yes, 'the mind is its own place;' and if it will keep that place, all doors will be opened from it." This ideal poor man must be "religious, wise, dignified, and humble, grasping at nothing, claiming all; willing to wait, never willing to give up; servile to none, the servant of all, — esteeming it the glory of a man to serve." Such a type of character, she tells us, is rare, but not unattainable.

The poems in this volume may be termed fugitive pieces, rhymes twined and dropped in the pathway of a life too busy for much versification. They somewhat recall Mr. Emerson's manner, but have not the point and felicity which have made him scarcely less eminent in verse than in prose. They will, however, well repay a perusal. In order that this volume may not be wholly lacking in their grace, we subjoin two short poems, which we have chosen from among a number of perhaps equal interest. One of these apostrophizes an artist whose rendering of her Greeks made him dear to her : —

FLAXMAN.

We deemed the secret lost, the spirit gone,
Which spake in Greek simplicity of thought,
And in the forms of gods and heroes wrought
Eternal beauty from the sculptured stone, —

A higher charm than modern culture won
With all the wealth of metaphysic lore,
Gifted to analyze, dissect, explore.
A many-colored light flows from one sun;
Art, 'neath its beams, a motley thread has spun;
The prism modifies the perfect day;
But thou hast known such mediums to shun,
And cast once more on life a pure, white ray.
Absorbed in the creations of thy mind,
Forgetting daily self, my truest self I find.

The other poem interprets for us the significance of one of the few jewels which queenly
Margaret deigned to wear, — a signet ring, bearing the image of Mercury: —

MY SEAL-RING.

Mercury has cast aside
The signs of intellectual pride,
Freely offers thee the soul:
Art thou noble to receive?
Canst thou give or take the whole,
Nobly promise, and believe?
Then thou wholly human art,
A spotless, radiant ruby heart,
And the golden chain of love
Has bound thee to the realm above.
If there be one small, mean doubt,
One serpent thought that fled not out,
Take instead the serpent-rod, —
Thou art neither man nor God.
Guard thee from the powers of evil, —
Who cannot trust, vows to the devil.
Walk thy slow and spell-bound way;
Keep on thy mask, or shun the day, —
Let go my hand upon the way.

INDEX.

University Press: John Wilson & Son, Cambridge.